Liberty and Justice for All

Liberty and Justice for All

Public Interest Law
in the 1980s and Beyond

Nan Aron

with a foreword by
Shirley M. Hufstedler

Westview Press
BOULDER & LONDON

Published in 1989 in the United States of America by Westview Press, Inc., 5500 Central Avenue, Boulder, Colorado 80301

Library of Congress Cataloging-in-Publication Data
Aron, Nan.
   Liberty and justice for all.
   Includes index.
   1. Public interest law—United States. I. Title.
KF390.5.P78A96 1989   349.73   88-17396
ISBN 0-8133-0696-5 347.3
ISBN 0-8133-1015-6 (pbk)

Printed and bound in the United States of America

The paper used in this publication meets the requirements of the American National Standard for Permanence of Paper for Printed Library Materials Z39.48-1984.

10   9   8   7   6   5   4   3   2   1

Contents

Tables and Figures

Foreword

"Liberty and justice for all" has been an expression of pious hope in America rather than a reality since the Republic was founded. Until well into this century, civil courts were primarily employed to settle the property disputes of the gentry, and criminal courts functioned to punish the transgressions of the unrepresented poor. In the past fifty years, countless people have struggled to transform millions of Americans' forlorn hopes for justice into real access to the justice system. It is doubtful that these changes would have happened without the efforts of public interest firms. Public interest lawyers opened the doors of courtrooms and legislatures to speak for those who were given no speaking parts and to speak for interests that will ever be speechless.

Despite the impact of public interest lawyers on society in general and on the justice system in particular, there is no book compiling the recent history of public interest law, describing the persons and institutions who practice it, and explaining how they do what they do. That is, there was none until Nan Aron wrote *Liberty and Justice for All: Public Interest Law in the 1980s and Beyond.* This book does all of that and more.

Liberty and Justice for All gives encouragement to law students to enter the field of public interest law. It is useful for anyone interested in American institutions; it is indispensable for those who practice with, for, or against public advocacy organizations. Finally, *Liberty and Justice for All* alerts the general public to the significant contribution of public interest lawyers to improving the quality of the decisions affecting all of our lives.

Shirley M. Hufstedler

AN ALLIANCE FOR JUSTICE BOOK

Alliance for Justice
Board of Directors

Acknowledgments

The intention of this book is to provide a better understanding of the mission of public interest lawyers and stimulate thought about ways to energize and build a movement that advances social justice. I could not have succeeded in this effort without the help and support of many individuals and institutions. I wish to express my appreciation for their assistance. I am very grateful to the Board of Directors of the Alliance for Justice for its wisdom in establishing the Alliance and for its continuing support for this book and other important projects.

I profited from discussion with many public interest lawyers, activists and foundation officers. These individuals, who are listed in Appendix D, gave generously of their time. A few merit special attention. Charles Halpern and the staff at the Council for Public Interest Law, who wrote *Balancing the Scales of Justice: Financing Public Interest Law in America,* provided a wonderful model for me to follow.

I am grateful to Susan Kalish, who helped prepare some of the chapters, and to Monica Hauck for conducting the survey of public interest law firms. Nancy Broff, David Cohen, Frances Dubrowski, Henry Fleisher, Chester Hartman, Leslie Proll, and William Taylor gave useful advice and ideas. I thank Mary Searcy and Janet Lieberman for not only their help with proofreading and typing the manuscript but also their good humor. Joel Thomas and Muriel Ebitz were responsible for preparing the figures. David Altschuler provided invaluable assistance in analyzing the data survey. Finally, Veida Dehmlow deserves special thanks for copyediting the manuscript.

Several foundations made it possible for the Alliance to undertake this effort. They include the Aetna Life and Casualty, The Field, New-Land, Norman, and Charles H. Revson Foundations, and Rockefeller Family Associates. However, the views expressed and statements made in the book are solely my responsibility.

Finally, I owe special thanks to my family, Bernie, Nick, Emma, and Elena, without whose contribution this book would have been finished much sooner, but without whose support and encouragement it might not have been finished at all.

Nan Aron

INTRODUCTION

Public Interest Law: An Essential Component of the American Legal System

- In a 1984 precedent-setting case involving the Erwin nuclear processing plant in Tennessee—a facility that was leaking hazardous PCBs, cyanide, and mercury into the surrounding environment— the Natural Resources Defense Council forced the Department of Energy to comply with federal hazardous waste laws at all national nuclear weapons facilities.
- In a significant 1986 case, *Meritor Savings Bank v. Vinson,* the Supreme Court ruled that businesses may be held liable for sexual harassment by supervisors, even if the company has not been informed of the conduct and the harassment has no economic impact on the victim. The case was championed by public interest groups such as the Women's Legal Defense Fund and the National Women's Law Center.
- In 1982, as a result of an administrative petition filed by Public Advocates, Inc., the Food and Drug Administration and the Department of Health and Human Services required manufacturers of infant formula to place pictorial instructions on formula packages. The pictures enabled illiterate parents to prepare the formula and helped eliminate infant health problems associated with its improper use.
- In a petition filed with the New York State Attorney General's office, the Center for Science in the Public Interest called on the state to enforce ingredients labeling laws with regard to fast food chains. The petition served as the catalyst for announcements by McDonald's and Burger King in 1986 that they would disclose ingredients information in their restaurants. The Attorney General's office described the decision as "unprecedented" and an essential public health measure.

- The National Organization for Women (NOW) Legal Defense and Education Fund joined the State of Minnesota in persuading the Supreme Court in 1984 to allow full membership to women in the Jaycees. Before the Court issued its opinion in *Roberts v. U.S. Jaycees,* the Jaycees had limited women to second-class membership, and did not permit them to vote or hold office. The decision set an example for other clubs throughout the country.
- A 1984 study by the Children's Defense Fund revealed that one out of three American children lives in poverty. The story received widespread coverage in leading newspapers and magazines, fueling public debate on the welfare of children and mapping out legal strategies for the future.

These examples demonstrate public interest law's increasing breadth and importance in American society. Through litigation, public education, community organizing, and lobbying efforts, public interest lawyers pursue causes that would otherwise go unrepresented. In the words of Supreme Court Justice Thurgood Marshall:

Public interest law seeks to fill some of the gaps in our legal system. Today's public interest lawyers have built upon the earlier successes of civil rights, civil liberties, and legal aid lawyers, but have moved into new areas. Before courts, administrative agencies and legislatures, they provide representation for a broad range of relatively powerless minorities—for example, to the mentally ill, to children, to the poor of all races. They also represent neglected interests that are widely shared by most of us as consumers, as workers, and as individuals in need of privacy and a healthy environment. These lawyers have, I believe, made an important contribution. They do not (nor should they) always prevail, but they have won many important victories for their clients. More fundamentally, perhaps, they have made our legal process work better. They have broadened the flow of information to decision-makers. They have made it possible for administrators, legislators, and judges to assess the impact of their decisions in terms of all affected interests. And, by helping open doors to our legal system, they have moved us a little closer to the ideal of equal justice for all.[1]

Public interest lawyers have increased society's recognition of the rights of minorities, women, consumers, poor people, and other disadvantaged segments of society. They have played an important role in the evolution of laws protecting the environment and making the workplace safer. By fighting to make government more accountable and business more responsible, public interest law has carved out a niche for itself in the system of checks and balances that underlies a pluralistic society.

DEFINING PUBLIC INTEREST LAW

Public interest law is the name given to efforts to provide legal representation to interests that historically have been unrepresented or underrepresented in the legal process. Philosophically, public interest law rests on the assumption that many significant segments of society are not adequately represented in the courts, Congress, or the administrative agencies, because they are either too poor or too diffuse to obtain legal representation in the marketplace.

A "public interest law organization" describes traditional civil rights and civil liberties organizations as well as firms that provide representation to consumers, environmentalists, and workers concerned about health and safety. Within this universe, the Alliance for Justice has made a further distinction. Programs that focus on policy-oriented cases, where a decision will advance a major law reform objective or affect large numbers of people, are discussed in this book. Such organizations comprise the membership of the Alliance, which was established to address broad generic issues which affect their funding and survival.

On the other hand are programs whose primary function is serving a large number of individual clients on a wide variety of matters. These include legal aid societies, public defenders, and legal services offices, which are not therefore the focus of this book.

In the early 1970s, when *Balancing the Scales of Justice: Financing Public Interest Law in America,* a report by the Council for Public Interest Law, was published, the term "public interest law" applied to a self-contained, easily definable, and relatively homogeneous set of organizations. In response to the widely held belief that public policy was too often shaped by corporations and other interests with substantial resources, consumer and environmental groups emerged to represent citizens in the courts and to administrative agencies.

Another set of organizations, founded during the late 1960s and early 1970s, addresses problems in public institutions such as prisons and hospitals for the mentally ill and provides legal representation to prisoners and institutionalized mental patients. Such facilities frequently operate outside the purview of the public and press, as well as out of reach of the legislators who were responsible for their oversight.

Public interest groups, together with the civil rights and civil liberties organizations which preceded them, share an enthusiasm for using the legal system to redress social and economic injustices. Influenced by the activism of the antiwar, civil rights, feminist, and environmental movements of the late 1960s and early 1970s, public interest lawyers have developed a common set of goals: to make government more accountable to the public and more responsive to the concerns and needs of unrepresented persons; to increase the power of citizens' groups; to insist on a place at the bargaining table; and to ensure that the development of public policy be open to public scrutiny.

Public interest groups have been tagged "liberal" because they were originally identified with causes generally regarded as such. Today, public interest law can no longer be thought of as a monolithic movement dedicated to any one political agenda. It is practiced by organizations that span the ideological spectrum. Groups calling themselves public interest law firms, such as the Pacific, the Mountain States, and the Mid-American Legal Foundations have become increasingly visible and active in pushing a conservative program. The Reagan administration shared their pro-development, anti-environmental, and anti-consumer views, and many of their founders and members, such as James Watt, became directors of government agencies. While focusing almost exclusively on the needs and concerns of the business community, these groups nonetheless operate under the mantle of a public interest law firm and benefit from its favorable tax-exempt status.

PUBLIC INTEREST LAW ORGANIZATIONS

In this book, the term "public interest law center" includes public interest law programs set up as tax-exempt entities. Generally, they are independent corporations under the supervision of a board of trustees, funded chiefly by foundation grants and contributions from the public. To obtain tax exemption as a charitable organization, they must satisfy the Internal Revenue Service's (IRS) criteria for public interest law firms, which are based on the idea that the *sine qua non* of public interest law is to provide underrepresented groups with access to the legal system.

Also included in the category of public interest law groups are those programs funded primarily by the government. The Legal Services Corporation's special support centers, known as back-up centers, provide legal services to the poor in areas where specialized legal knowledge is required.

The book does not survey the private public interest bar, primarily because of the difficulty in developing a comprehensive listing of the firms, solo practitioners, and law professors involved in this type of practice. Nevertheless, these lawyers are a vital source of new ideas and experimentation in the delivery of legal services and handle hundreds of civil rights, civil liberties, and environmental and consumer protection cases each year. Because of the importance of their contributions, the book occasionally draws upon their work and experiences.

PUBLIC INTEREST LAW TODAY

Economic hardship has been a fact of life for public interest groups since their inception. Committed to defending interests that by definition cannot afford to pay lawyers market rates and prohibited by IRS rules from accepting client fees of any sort, public interest legal organizations have always had to depend on funds provided by philanthropic and public sources. They will never be wholly self-supporting, and, despite their impressive track record, are by no means assured of a continued place in the American legal system. For these reasons, it is essential that the organized bar, law schools, government officials, foundation officers, and the public renew their interest in and support of the public interest law movement.

THE CURRENT STATUS OF PUBLIC INTEREST LAW

Nurtured by an outpouring of foundation funding and stimulated by the emergence of a variety of new social movements, the public interest legal community grew rapidly in the 1960s and early 1970s. By 1975, the Council for Public Interest Law had identified almost 600 public interest lawyers practicing in over 60 tax-exempt public interest law centers. By 1979, the number of centers had risen to 110. The results of the Alliance for Justice's 1983–84 survey of public interest law centers demonstrate the resiliency of the public interest movement in the hostile environment of the 1980s. Despite inflation, defunding by foundations and the government, attacks on its legitimacy from New Right spokespersons, and attempts by the Reagan administration to undermine the charitable status of its activities, the public interest legal community has continued to grow in size, in diversity of activities, and in influence. The late-1980s present a particularly opportune time to re-examine the nature and mission of public interest law. This book discusses its changing issues and strategies and develops a set of recommendations for its survival and growth.

Notes

1. "Financing Public Interest Law: The Role of the Organized Bar." Address by Justice Thurgood Marshall to the Award of Merit Luncheon of the Bar Activities Section of the American Bar Association, August 10, 1975.

1

History of Public Interest Law

There is hardly a political question in the United States which does not sooner or later turn into a judicial one.[1]

Consumers were the bugs on the Reagan windshield of regulatory removal. With all the subtlety of Jane Byrne clearing the snowbound streets of Chicago in an election year, the Reagan regulators set to work plowing up the national framework of regulation.[2]

THE ROOTS OF PUBLIC INTEREST LAW

Although the term "public interest law" was coined no more than two decades ago, it is not a new phenomenon. Public interest law is the outgrowth of diverse efforts stretching deep into American history to secure legal representation for the powerless and disenfranchised. The legal aid movement of the 1800s, Progessive Era reformers such as Louis Brandeis, the civil liberties activism of the American Civil Liberties Union (ACLU) in the early 1900s, the watershed civil rights cases of the 1950s—these are some of the roots of public interest law. As Tulane law professor Oliver Houck observed in a recent *Yale Law Journal* article:

> These three large movements in poverty, civil liberties, and civil rights practice changed more than the law of their respective fields. As they evolved, particularly into the 1960s, these organizations changed the way lawyers approached the law. Their lawyers had clients and the clients were injured, but so also was a larger sense of justice which is as difficult to define precisely as it would be to deny. Most importantly, they did not simply seek compensation for their clients; increasingly they sought to change the law.[3]

Public interest law as it flowered in the 1970s owed its patterns of organization, modes of financing, and choices of strategies to the diverse predecessors described below.

6

The Legal Aid Movement

Organized legal aid for the poor in this country began in 1876 with the establishment of a program of legal assistance for recently arrived immigrants by the German Society of New York. By the turn of the century, there were six cities with legal aid organizations. By 1917 there were forty-one, and by 1940 there were over fifty.[4]

Legal aid differed from the *pro bono* work that might occasionally be taken on by sympathetic lawyers of the day in that it was an institutionalized response to need—a social service subsidized by a third party. Legal aid efforts embraced the people who have no access to legal services in the marketplace and demonstrated how these people could be served. Legal aid's service and charitable orientation is distinct from the policy-making and legal reform emphasis of modern public interest law.[5]

However, the organizational form used by legal aid is the forerunner of today's public interest law firm: an independent private office, separate from any commercial law firm, with salaried lawyers working full time on the problems of a client population that otherwise would lack access to legal representation. The idea, first articulated by Reginald Heber Smith in 1919,[6] that the organized bar should help finance legal aid activities to discharge the collective social responsibility of the legal profession, is a concept critical to the funding of public interest law today.

The Progressive Legacy

Around the turn of the twentieth century, the courts became a battleground where new protective labor and consumer legislation, which created federal regulatory agencies such as the Federal Trade Commission, came up against legal doctrines that defended unregulated business enterprise. During this time of rapid industrialization and social and political change, Progressive Era leaders secured general acceptance of the principle that government should intervene in the economic life of society to see that the market does not operate in a way injurious to the public welfare. This principle, under attack in recent years, is a bulwark of public interest law.

Louis Brandeis—attorney, presidential adviser, and Supreme Court Justice—exemplified the public-spirited, policy-minded advocates of the Progressive Era. Brandeis believed that the law must not "sacrifice the interests of the public to a single corporation."[7] He urged that courts and administrative bodies alike consider the public interest when making decisions and forming policy. He involved himself in legal battles over such issues as antitrust policy, protective labor legislation, and the conservation of federal wilderness lands in Alaska.[8] Brandeis also urged lawyers to recognize that as members of an economic, intellectual, and managerial elite, they had a social obligation to act as more than the "adjuncts of great corporations."[9]

In one sense, the views of Brandeis and the Progressives are similar to those of most contemporary public interest lawyers. Both believe that government has an obligation to respond to changing public needs and interests, and that lawyers have an obligation to consider the social implications of their work. However, the two groups differ over the proper role of the judiciary. The Progressives, while emphasizing the role of lawyers and legal action, nonetheless believed that legislatures and administrative agencies were the most effective vehicles for advancing the public interest and urged the courts to defer to these forums to resolve all social and economic matters. Modern public interest lawyers, however, have reacted against this view of a restrained judiciary and have used the courts to force agencies and institutions to comply with statutory and constitutional law.

The American Civil Liberties Union

Founded as a citizens' lobby designed to call public and governmental attention to violations of the First Amendment rights of pacifists and conscientious objectors during World War I, the ACLU is a direct antecedent of the public interest law firm. From the beginning, it relied on a variety of strategies—lobbying, litigating, grass roots organizing, educating the public, and using personal influence on sympathetic leaders—to oppose encroachments on the constitutional rights of individuals in cases primarily involving "sensitive issues of free speech, privacy, and due process."[10]

Working mainly through volunteer attorneys and often limited to an *amicus* or "friend of the court" role, the ACLU nonetheless has built a semi-autonomous network consisting of local affiliates in every state. The affiliates focus on local disputes that involve important questions of federal law and social policy, and this emphasis on national issues has become a major characteristic of subsequent public interest law organizations. The ACLU has also promoted the idea that government needs a watchdog, an outside citizen's organization to monitor its functions and guard against corruption and abuses of power.[11]

The NAACP Legal Defense and Education Fund

The civil rights movement is, in many ways, the crucible in which modern public interest law was forged. The public interest law firms that have worked on behalf of environmental, consumer, and many other issues since the 1960s owe much of their organization, strategy, and inspiration to the National Association for the Advancement of Colored People Legal Defense and Education Fund (NAACP/LDF) and its landmark victories in the 1950s and 1960s.

In the 1930s, the NAACP, founded two decades earlier, took a significant step in the evolution of public interest law. It initiated "a comprehensive campaign against the major disabilities from which Negros suffer in American life—legal, political, and economic."[12] The NAACP developed a legal strategy, a long-term litigation campaign that concentrated on eliminating racial segregation in education, employment, and housing based on the notion that the "separate-but-equal" doctrine was unworkable because separate facilities are inherently unequal. The NAACP/LDF, established as a separate entity in 1939, worked in concert with its parent organization to win the precedent-setting school desegregation decision, *Brown v. Board of Education*, before the Supreme Court in 1954. *Brown* was used to build a chain of decisions that eventually eliminated the legal basis for segregation in public facilities.

These legal victories in turn fostered a political climate that permitted the establishment of a federal Commission on Civil Rights in 1958 and the passage of the Civil Rights Act of 1964, which created a statutory basis for the federal enforcement of equality in education, employment, and public accommodations.

Another landmark case, *NAACP v. Button* (1963) removed potential legal obstacles to the practice of public interest law. The Supreme Court rejected attempts by the State of Virginia to prevent attorneys working with the NAACP/LDF from seeking out and providing representation on questions with clear political importance. *Button* made it possible for civil rights groups and later public interest lawyers to seek out clients and openly use litigation as a part of a broad strategy of reform. It also made it easier for subsequent public interest law centers to treat the law strategically.

To organize and perform its work, raise funds, and institutionalize victories, the NAACP/LDF developed an organizational model that today is used in one form or another by virtually all public interest law endeavors. The main features of this model are as follows:

- Like legal aid societies, the organization uses a full-time salaried staff of highly qualified lawyers rather than relying on volunteers or counsel hired on an *ad hoc* basis.
- Unlike legal aid societies, but like the ACLU, the organization does not handle routine "service" cases in which the matter is of

concern only to those who are directly affected by the question at issue.

- The organization rejects a reactive or defensive posture in representing the client's interest, instead assuming an active role in the strategic accomplishment of goals. Litigation serves as a primary tool for initiating changes in the way in which political and social institutions deal with minority interests.
- The organization depends for its primary financial support upon a widespread national membership of concerned citizens that gives small sums to support the work of the organization, even though it serves a very special, relatively poor, interest group.
- The organization rejects the simple accumulation of big cases in favor of a series of incremental victories that create a favorable legal climate while fostering a public concern that may convert victories in the courts into a change in public policy.
- The organization works through a self-generated network of cooperating private attorneys to follow up victories achieved to convert theoretical statutory rights into practical substantive benefits.

This model has proved successful with a variety of subsequent public interest law endeavors. With it the NAACP/LDF demonstrated that it is possible for a minority group not merely to challenge the constitutionality of individual statutes or policies, but also to build an agenda for change that can shift the political system into positive action and may, at the same time, erode the legal ground under the opposition.

The public interest law activity that burgeoned in so many issue areas in the 1960s and 1970s was not such a departure from the past as some have assumed. In many ways it has resembled the process of pouring new wine into old bottles. The goal of providing legal representation on behalf of those who cannot obtain service in the marketplace, the organizational framework of an office of staffed attorneys, the subsidized financing, the watchdog role over the government, the often adversarial role *vis-à-vis* business interests, the strategy of planned legal reform, and the close linkage of litigation with a broad range of other organizing and educational activities to effect social change—all these elements of today's practice of public interest law have their beginnings decades and even generations ago.

EXPANSION OF PUBLIC INTEREST LAW

The 1960s and 1970s were a time of ferment and change. The civil rights and the antiwar struggles drew many ordinary citizens into political and social activism. At the same time, the publication of such books as Rachel Carson's *Silent Spring* and Ralph Nader's *Unsafe At Any Speed* heightened public awareness of the potential hazards involved in everyday applications of the technologies of the post–World War II era. The emergence of many social movements—providing greater opportunity for poor people, preserving the environment, protecting consumers, and ending employment discrimination against minorities and women—channeled the restless energies of the era into efforts to achieve social justice. The law was a major focus for these constituencies, just as it had been for the NAACP/LDF and the ACLU in earlier decades. Lobbying for new laws and litigating cases to ensure that existing protections were enforced by government agencies became components of an overall social reform strategy for these groups.

The Role of Private Foundations

The late 1960s and the early 1970s saw a great proliferation of public interest law activity. This growth was fostered by the increase in foundation support; previously the philanthropic community had been hesitant to venture into granting funds to law-related programs. Foundations began to fund civil rights organizations and a whole spectrum of consumer, environmental, and multi-issue public interest law firms. The willingness of philanthropists to support organizations that proposed to use the law to advance new causes was crucial to the rapid development of new public interest law centers such as the Center for Law and Social Policy, the Center for Law in the Public Interest, the Citizens Communication Center, the Institute for Public Representation, the Natural Resources Defense Council, Public Advocates, Inc., and the Sierra Club Legal Defense Fund.[13]

The Role of Federal Government

Many major government initiatives of the 1960s and 1970s helped create a climate that was conducive to the growth of public interest law. The War on Poverty stimulated legal aid efforts; the Office of Economic Opportunity established a Legal Services Program in the mid-1960s, which in 1974 became an independent public corporation. Citizens' groups and their lawyers lobbied Congress to enact new laws in civil rights, environmental, and consumer areas. They also urged the adoption of new federal programs and the establishment of new executive branch agencies to deal with their concerns.

During this period, Congress recognized that many of these civil rights and consumer statutes depended heavily on private enforcement. To encourage the private bar to take these cases, Congress enacted legislation mandating the award of legal fees and expenses for plaintiffs who prevail in public interest litigation. These counsel fees statutes would also benefit the public interest lawyer, who, stated a district court judge in a 1972 environmental case in California, acts as a "private attorney general," supplementing government's efforts in enforcing and implementing these laws.[14]

Congress, lobbied by many different interests, found it difficult to resolve all issues through legislation and increasingly deferred to administrative agencies. The proceedings of federal regulatory agencies, formerly limited primarily to the participation of the agencies and the businesses they regulated, were opened to citizen organizations through a 1966 court case involving the Federal Communications Commission. This case "assert[ed] the right of public interest groups to separate representation in the proceedings of government agencies even though the agency itself may have been established specifically to represent the public."[15]

The Internal Revenue Service's (IRS) recognition of public interest law as a charitable activity under section 501(c)(3) of the tax code led to further consolidation of the practice. Historically, the IRS never questioned the status of traditionally charitable groups such as the NAACP/LDF, the ACLU, and the National Wildlife Federation. There was never any doubt in the agency's mind that these organizations qualified as charitable. The same was not true, however, for some of the newer public interest law centers. Official recognition that they were legitimate 501(c)(3) organizations occurred in the fall of 1970, after a storm of public controversy following the IRS's October announcement temporarily suspending the granting of charitable, tax-exempt status to such centers. The Service's definition of a charitable public interest law firm allowed access to the legal system for interests that could not secure private representation. IRS guidelines provided, among other rules, that a charitable public interest law firm can under no circumstances accept fees from clients,[16] must account to the IRS as to why the cases on its docket further the public interest, and must be directed by a citizen board independent of substantial private interests.

Thus, what apparently began as a challenge to the legitimacy of public interest law firms ended by reinforcing their legal underpinnings as charitable, tax-exempt organizations. This vindication of their charitable status was important for public interest law firms. As Oliver Houck pointed out:

> The Code declares in effect, and history concurs, that these organizations do good works. They wear white hats. In the marketplace for

giving—public, corporate and foundation—this imprimatur goes a long way. . . . [17]

The Role of the Private Bar and the Law Schools

The private bar and the law schools were also involved in the emergence of public interest law during the 1970s. Many lawyers volunteered their services to work with the NAACP/LDF, the ACLU, the Lawyers' Committee for Civil Rights Under Law, and other public interest law organizations. An increasing number of lawyers saw public interest activities as a way for the legal profession to discharge its social responsibility, a way "the professional ethic of the private bar [can] expand to incorporate a concept of service to the public."[18] At least for a time, the opportunity to perform a substantial amount of pro bono work on firm time was a powerful lure for many talented young law school graduates. During this time many law schools developed internship and clinical education programs, several of them funded by the Council for Legal Education for Professional Responsibility, a grant-making organization established by the Ford Foundation.[19]

Part of the American Legal System

Building upon these events, public interest law established itself in the 1960s and 1970s, and gradually matured and became institutionalized. "Fifteen years after the new generation of public interest law was born, the turbulent practice has survived to become a permanent fixture on the American legal landscape," wrote Fred Strasser in a 1985 *National Law Journal* article.[20]

However, with influence has come controversy. Michael Pertschuk, former Commissioner of the Federal Trade Commission, referred to the consumer law movement as a "disturber of the peace."[21] Affected business groups, for example, have complained about "excess" proceduralism involved in the preparation of environmental impact statements, leading to delays in building projects ranging from the Alaska pipeline to atomic energy plants. In addition, court decrees increasing opportunities for minorities and women, creating new legal rights for the poor, and remedying conditions in public institutions have stirred up opposition among certain vocal segments to the causes advanced by public interest lawyers.

This backlash coincided with the swing of the political pendulum to the right. The election of Ronald Reagan in 1980 created a dramatic break with the past and ushered in a new era of less federal responsibility and protection for the poor and disadvantaged.

THE PENDULUM SWINGS TO THE RIGHT

The political philosophy of the Reagan Administration called for a drastic reduction in the domestic role of the federal government. Reagan Administration officials wanted to limit social spending, reduce government regulation, and cut programs for disadvantaged groups. They disapproved of many of the social initiatives of the sixties and seventies and were openly hostile to the public interest organizations that had been instrumental in achieving those initiatives.

President Reagan took his efforts to change the role of government to Congress, the administrative and regulatory agencies, and the Supreme Court. He initiated a three-pronged strategy: slashing the budgets of federal agencies; appointing agency officials sympathetic with the Administration's overall mission; and lobbying Congress to overturn environmental, consumer, and civil rights statutes. Under the banner of "defunding the left," President Reagan also sought to cut off sources of public funding for public interest and legal services organizations and to vitiate the working relationship that had developed over the years between these groups and various branches of government.

Former Senator Thomas F. Eagleton's description of President Reagan's attempts to kill the Legal Services program aptly sums up the Administration's overall strategy: "There are three ways to kill a program, and the President with respect to Legal Services has tried all three. One way is to kill it outright. That didn't succeed. Another is to fund it at such a low level as to make it inoperative. From Reagan's point of view he made a little progress on that, he got the budget cut. And the third way is to put the management and the oversight of the program in unfriendly hands."[22]

The Executive Branch

Ronald Reagan came into office suspicious of the regulatory bureaucracy and quickly moved to contain it. In making appointments to the federal commissions and regulatory agencies, President Reagan often chose leaders who were openly hostile to the historic mission or even to the continued existence of their offices. Such was the case with the appointment of William Harvey to the Legal Services Corporation, Clarence Pendleton to the Civil Rights Commission, Anne Burford to the Environmental Protection Agency, and James Watt to the Department of the Interior.

In some instances, federal officials adopted positions directly contradictory to those taken in preceding decades. For example, Ronald Reagan's close associates, Attorneys General William French Smith and, later, Edwin Meese, urged the abandonment of numerical goals in minority hiring and promotions as a remedy for job discrimination; petitioned the Supreme Court to reverse the *Roe v. Wade* decision permitting abortion; attempted to undermine numerous affirmative action consent decrees entered into by civil rights plaintiffs, businesses, and local governments; and urged in the *Bob Jones* case that the IRS reverse its twelve-year policy of denying tax exemptions to racially discriminatory educational institutions.

Reagan appointees, opposed to government regulation, quickly weakened the oversight role of the administrative agencies. For instance, Dr. Sidney M. Wolfe, Director of Public Citizen's Health Research Group, criticized the Food and Drug Administration's (FDA) lax enforcement of health and safety laws, stating that the agency's approach under President Reagan was reminiscent of "an era before the 1900s, when industry was self-regulating."[23]

Governmental inaction became a particularly severe problem in the area of environmental protection. "The enforcement of environmental laws by the the executive branch has all too frequently been weak and grudging," stated Frederic P. Sutherland, director of the Sierra Club Legal Defense Fund. "The agencies and officials charged with administering the laws have delayed, missed deadlines, attempted to convert mandatory standards to discretionary ones, created loopholes, watered down strict statutes through the use of the regulatory process, or simply refused to use their enforcement powers when faced with blatant violations of law." Under such circumstances, the watchdog role of public interest lawyers becomes crucial.[24] One of the president's first acts in office was to sign an executive order that gave increased authority to the Office of Management and Budget (OMB), transforming the agency into what some critics referred to as a "regulatory czar." OMB had the power to review all regulations issued by executive agencies and to postpone implementation of or rescind rules that business groups viewed as too stringent or costly.[25]

A report issued by the Alliance For Justice in 1981 entitled *Contempt for Law* detailed the process by which numerous public health, environmental, and civil rights regulations were relaxed or vetoed through OMB's intervention. The report charged that, through OMB, the Reagan Administration went much further than previous administrations in acceding to the demands of business in formulating policy. The result has been, in the words of Alexander Schmidt, FDA Commissioner under President Nixon, "more politicization . . . than . . . warranted by rational politics or good for the American people. Decisions once made largely on scientific merits are increasingly subject to political considerations . . . and the recommendations of career staff are increasingly overruled to reflect the Reagan Administration's philosophy of more government accommodation to industry."[26]

One effect of these developments was low morale and a high attrition rate among experienced personnel in the executive agencies. A 1982 *New York Times* article described the atmosphere in the particularly troubled Environmental Protection Agency: "There is a deep sense that [the] management team distrusts the professional staff. Agency veterans have watched as a destructive 'we-them' attitude has supplanted the strong feeling of unity and shared goals that typified E.P.A. for more than a decade." At the same time, an "increase in work [load] and the budget cut[s have] . . . spread available resources so thin . . . that activities proceed at a snail's pace, if at all."[27]

Similar morale and productivity problems permeated the entire federal bureaucracy, and the Reagan Administration witnessed a substantial decrease in expertise as many dedicated career civil servants left or were forced out. The federal agencies which once attracted lawyers and advocates committed to public service lost much of their appeal. Consequently, public interest legal groups assumed a large part of the responsibility for carrying out the work that government used to perform.

The Legislative Branch

The Administration also pursued its mission through the legislative branch. Although meeting with some resistance in Congress, the Reagan Administration was generally successful in shifting federal spending priorities. The federal budget as a whole was not reduced, due to the increase in defense spending, but funds for social services were sharply cut. However, the burden of cuts was uneven. The large "entitlement" programs such as Social Security grew, while most other human services spending, including aid to the poor, decreased: non-entitlement social spending fell $70 billion (14 percent) between 1982 and 1986.[28]

The federal budget cuts were particularly severe for social services, employment and training programs, community development activities, legal services, health programs other than Medicare and Medicaid, elementary and secondary education, and environmental programs. Spending reductions thus targeted many of the issues and the constituencies of public interest organizations: they also threatened the funding base of many of the groups themselves.

The Reagan Administration was less successful, however, in persuading Congress to repeal the environmental, consumer, and civil rights statutes that had been passed in the preceding twenty years. Congress resisted attempts to weaken the Clean Air, Clean Water, Consumer Product Safety, and Voting Rights Acts.

Several Reagan-initiated bills attempted to weaken the institutional arrangements that had enabled public interest law to become a prominent force for reform. The proposed "court-stripping" legislation, introduced in 1986 by Senator Orrin Hatch, an ally of the president, would have forbidden the courts from using race as a factor in determining pupil assignment to public schools, making court-ordered desegregation plans impossible. Another Hatch-sponsored proposal, the Legal Fees Equity Act, would have capped at well below market rates the legal fees awarded to public interest lawyers when they prevail in litigation against governmental entities. President Reagan also opposed the Equal Access to Justice Act, which allows individuals, small businesses, and nonprofit groups to recover attorneys' fees through court awards if a government action against them is determined to be "not sufficiently justified." Although vetoed by the president in 1984, the act was signed into law the following year.

Congress refused to accede to Administration attempts to abolish the Legal Services Corporation (LSC) with its more than 1200 field offices serving poor people, and several legal "support centers" specializing in various aspects of poverty law. From the beginning of his Administration, every year President Reagan tried to eliminate the LSC through budget proposals calling for zero-level funding. Congress repeatedly denied his request, and continued to appropriate money for the Corporation.

The Reagan Administration's legislative program fell short of its stated goals primarily because they were too far to the right of the existing political consensus. In many cases, the actions proposed were so extreme that they alienated even conservative allies in Congress.

The Judicial Branch

To institutionalize the Reagan revolution, the Administration pushed and argued its policies in the courts. A sharp change in tone and direction within the Justice Department marked Edwin Meese's tenure as Attorney General. Far more activist than his predecessor, William French Smith, Mr. Meese fashioned a far-reaching agenda: to persuade the courts to adopt the Administration's positions on abortion, school prayer, affirmative action, and busing.

Working with Mr. Meese, the Solicitor General filed an unprecedented number of *amicus* briefs which aggressively pressed President Reagan's social agenda. In 1985, for example, Charles Fried filed nearly twice as many *amicus* briefs as his predecessor did.[29] Another crucial part of Mr. Meese's program was to reduce civil rights litigation, a task he delegated to Assistant Attorney General for Civil Rights William Bradford Reynolds, a political appointee actively opposed to equal rights for women and minorities.

The Administration's most ambitious task and enduring legacy was the reshaping of the federal bench. In addition to his Supreme Court appointments, President Reagan named close to half of the nation's 743 federal judges by the end of his second term. By selecting judges who shared his conservative ideology, he sought to overturn decisions that resulted from the liberal "judicial activism" of the 1960s and 1970s and to ensure that his social philosophy would last well into the twenty-first century. According to Mario Moreno, Associate Counsel of the Mexican American Legal Defense and Educational Fund, "The Administration applied a rigid ideological litmus test by nominating individuals who favor 'judicial restraint' and support the Administration's position on abortion, school prayer, death penalty and affirmative action."[30]

Underscoring the ideological nature of Reagan's judicial appointments was the fact that a large number of appointees were drawn from conservative groups with close ties to the Reagan Administration. For example, many of President Reagan's judicial appointees were affiliated with the Federalist Society, a conservative network of lawyers in academia and government. Justice Antonin Scalia and Judges Ralph Winter, Stephen F. Williams, Robert Bork, Richard Posner, Frank Easterbrook, and John T. Noonan, Jr., were all Federalist Society members.[31]

At the state level, a well-financed campaign to unseat California Supreme Court Justices Cruz Reynoso, Rose Bird, and Joseph Grodin led voters to reject all three. According to Justice Grodin, the campaign was a "right wing attack" which seized upon the issue of the death penalty to arouse public opposition to the justices. It remains to be seen, says Grodin, whether the courts and the public will be exposed to similar experiences in the future.[32]

In summary, the Reagan Administration achieved some far-reaching changes in the way government operates, in the ideological cast of people in government, and in the national political climate. These actions made government a less vigorous protector of citizens and their rights and made it more difficult for advocates to work effectively with government. Citizens' groups in general and public interest legal centers in particular found themselves with enormous battles to fight in a much more hostile environment and a pinch in resources with which to operate.

ATTACKS ON PUBLIC INTEREST LAW ORGANIZATIONS

"Defund the left," a phrase popularized in a 1982 *New York Times* column by New Right fundraiser Richard Viguerie, became a rallying cry for the Reagan Administration in its early years. The most successful of its defunding strategies were the budget cuts, which affected not only progressive causes and organizations but many traditional service organizations and community groups as well. Another component of its overall strategy to stifle public interest groups was its effort to discredit the notion of advocacy and to make it more difficult for organizations to participate in the political process. However, in its zeal, the Administration used so broad a brush that its actions threatened not just public interest organizations but the entire nonprofit sector. As a result, President Reagan was forced to rescind many of his initiatives.

OMB Circular A-122

In early 1983, the Administration launched a major attack on citizen and community groups. It proposed changes in Circular A-122, an obscure cost-accounting regulation for government contractors, that defined as "political advocacy" any effort to "affect the opinions of the general public" or to communicate with state, local, or federal public officials. Even a copying machine in an office that was partially supported by public funds could not be used for "advocacy" purposes. The A-122 regulations would have effectively prevented the staff of organizations that received government funding from carrying out any lobbying or advocacy activities, even if they did so on their own time or used private funds.

With its far-reaching freedom of speech implications, the proposal created a storm of controversy, and a diverse coalition of groups—the Red Cross, Girl Scouts of America, the Aerospace Industries Association, Common Cause, the Chamber of Commerce, the National Association of Manufacturers, the Alliance for Justice, and others—came together to defeat it. The coalition succeeded in forcing OMB to make some changes in the circular. The new version was less extreme than the original, but still contained what the *New York Times* called "potentially chilling rules."[33]

Combined Federal Campaign

Under President Reagan, the Office of Personnel and Management (OPM) repeatedly attempted to oust public interest law groups from the Combined Federal Campaign (CFC), the annual workplace fund drive conducted for government employees. Through the donations of federal employees, the CFC raises hundreds of thousands of dollars for a wide range of charities including the United Way, the American Heart Association, and the Red Cross. In the 1970s, the CFC was opened to public interest groups such as the NAACP/LDF, the Wilderness Society, and the Mexican American Legal Defense and Educational Fund.

Reagan appointee Donald Devine, Director of OPM, issued an executive order and regulations in 1982 excluding "advocacy groups" from the campaign. The action led to a protracted battle. Public interest groups eventually won the right to participate in the campaign by successfully lobbying Congress to enact permanent legislation.

In spite of Administration rhetoric about separating public funding from private advocacy, there is much evidence that the real objective was to reduce government support of public interest organizations. For example, after an unsuccessful battle in 1981 to persuade Congress to abolish the Legal Services Corporation, the Corporation's Reagan-appointed leadership came under congressional fire in 1984 for making grants to such far-to-the-right groups as the Constitutional Law Center, the National Center for the Medically Dependent and Disabled Inc., and the Urban Legal Foundation. In criticizing these grants as inconsistent with LSC's mission to provide legal aid to the poor, Representative Barney Frank (D-Mass.) commented, "They've moved from defunding the left to funding the right."[34]

At a speech delivered at a Center for Law and Social Policy dinner, David Tatel, a lawyer in the Washington, D.C., firm of Hogan and Hartson, summarized the scope and impact of the Reagan initiatives on the public interest legal community:

What makes today's actions so different and so dangerous is that so many are aimed by all three branches of government at excluding minorities and the poor from the very processes of government where policy is made and which provide remedies for the violation of rights. The cuts in the legal services program and the severe limitations on its activities; the exclusion of entire classes of people from the judicial process through the application of narrowed principles of standing; the efforts to limit the advocacy rights of certain public interest organizations; and the narrowing and entirely inadequate antidiscrimination laws, are just a few examples of the kinds of actions which are making it increasingly difficult to participate in government and to obtain remedies for the violation of rights.[35]

To adjust to the changing economic and social climate, public interest law organizations altered their strategies and activities. They assumed many of the responsibilities abandoned by the government for fiscal or ideological reasons. Legal centers continued to use their resources to address environmental issues and to work for solutions to problems facing the poor, minorities, and consumers. At the same time, as explored more fully in Chapter 5, they were at the forefront of efforts to push the government to reassume its responsibilities and to open its procedures to greater public scrutiny.

Notes

1. Alexis de Tocqueville, *Democracy in America*. Ed. J.P. Mayer and Max Lerner, trans. George Lawrence (New York: Harper and Row, 1966), p. 248.

2. "The Coming of Age of the Public Interest Lobbyist." Address by Michael Pertschuk, former Federal Trade Commissioner, to the Political Science Forum, March 21, 1984.

3. Oliver A. Houck, "With Charity for All," 93 *Yale Law Journal* 8 (July 1984), p. 1441.

4. *Balancing the Scales of Justice: Financing Public Interest Law in America.* A report by the Council for Public Interest Law (Washington, D.C.: Council for Public Interest Law, 1976), pp. 21–22.

5. *The Public Interest Law Firm: New Voices for New Constituencies.* A report by the Ford Foundation (New York: The Ford Foundation, 1973), p. 7.

6. *Balancing*, p. 22.

7. Alpheus Mason, *Brandeis: A Free Man's Life.* (New York: Viking, 1946), p. 24.

8. *Ibid.*, p. 246–53, 282–89.

9. Louis Brandeis, "The Opportunity in the Law," *American Law Review* 39 (1905), p. 559.

10. Robert L. Rabin, "Lawyers for Social Change: Perspectives on Public Interest Law," 28 *Stanford Law Review* 210 (1976), p. 214.

11. *Balancing*, p. 32.

12. *Ibid.*, p. 33.

13. *New Voices*, pp. 20–25.

14. Judge Robert F. Peckham in *La Raza Unida v. Volpe*, as quoted in *New Voices*, p. 37.

15. *New Voices*, p. 9.

16. The Internal Revenue Service's decision to prohibit public interest law firms from accepting client fees "appears to have been based on three separate

considerations . . . First, the Service apparently believed that the receipt of client fees would be inconsistent with the articulated basis for the exemption of public interest law firms—providing legal representation on matters of public importance which is unavailable from commercial firms. Second, the Service sought to establish a clear distinction between exempt and taxable law firms and it chose client-paid fees as a significant distinguishing factor. Third, the Service presumably wanted to preclude any possibility of inurement of earnings to private individuals. Preventing the expectation of compensation from becoming a factor in case selection was apparently intended, in part, to accomplish that purpose." (Alliance for Justice interview with Sara-Ann Determan of Hogan & Hartson, March 24, 1980.)

17. Houck, "With Charity," pp. 1429–30.

18. David A. Marcello reviewing F. Raymond Marks, *et al.*, *The Lawyer, The Public, and Professional Responsibility* in 47 *Tulane Law Review* (1973), p. 944.

19. *New Voices*, pp. 18–19.

20. Fred Strasser, "Public Interest Law Acquires the Concerns of Middle Age," *National Law Journal*, vol. 7 (February 11, 1985), pp. 1, 8.

21. Michael Pertschuk, "The Consumer Movement in the Eighties: A Sleeping Giant Stirs." Speech to the Consumer Federation of America's Consumer Assembly, January 20, 1983.

22. Stuart Taylor, Jr., "Legal Aid for the Poor: Reagan's Longest Brawl," *New York Times*, June 8, 1984, p. A16.

23. Alan J. Abramson and Lester M. Salamon, *Nonprofits and the New Federal Budget.* (Washington, D.C.: The Urban Institute, 1986), p. 33.

24. Julie Kosterlitz, "Reagan Is Leaving His Mark on the Food and Drug Administration," *National Journal*, vol. 17, no. 3 (July 5, 1985), p. 1569.

25. Address by Frederic P. Sutherland, Director, Sierra Club Legal Defense Fund, to the National Affairs and Legislation and Conservation Committees of the Garden Club of America, October 8, 1984.

26. Cathy Catanzaro, "Tolchins Discuss 'Dismantling of America through Deregulation' at December WCL Luncheon," *Washington Council of Lawyers Newsletter*, January 1984, p. 3.

27. Kosterlitz, "Reagan Is Leaving His Mark," p. 1568.

28. John Jones and Jack Smith, "Critics of E.P.A. Are Right," *New York Times*, September 1, 1982, p. A23.

29. David O'Brien, "Meese's Agenda for Ensuring the Reagan Legacy," *Los Angeles Times*, September 28, 1986, p. 3.

30. Alliance for Justice interview with Mario Moreno, Associate Counsel of Mexican American Legal Defense and Educational Fund, January 9, 1986.

31. Steven G. Calabresi, "Judge Scalia's Cheerleaders," *New York Times*. July 23, 1986, p. B6.

32. Address by former California Supreme Court Justice Joseph R. Grodin at an Alliance for Justice symposium, "New Challenges in the Judicial Selection Process," February 2, 1987.

33. "Leave the 'Left' Alone" (editorial), *New York Times*, December 9, 1983, p. A34.

34. Stuart Taylor, Jr., "Congressmen Question Grants Made by Legal Services Unit," *New York Times*, October 22, 1984, p. A17.

35. Address by David Tatel at the 15th Anniversary Celebration of the Center for Law and Social Policy, October 3, 1984.

2

A Profile of Public Interest Law
Based on the 1983–84 Survey

He was a lawyer, yet not a rascal, and the people were astonished.[1]

Over the entrance to our Supreme Court Building in bold letters are chiseled the words, "Equal Justice Under Law." How wonderful it would be if we could in honesty say that we had achieved that great objective.[2]

SCOPE

Despite a hostile political climate and unusually adverse economic circumstances over the past few years, public interest legal organizations as a whole kept apace. An extensive survey of 158 groups carried out by the Alliance for Justice in 1983–84 shows, in general, an upward trend in public interest legal activity since surveys in 1975 and 1979. The number of groups has increased, the number of staff attorneys has grown, and there is greater variety in the issues these organizations address, the types of clients they serve, and the strategies they employ. Still, the political and economic strains of the 1980s have taken their toll on the public interest legal community. Although the number of centers has not declined, the rapid growth rate in this field recorded during the last decade has slowed markedly in recent years.

Prior to 1975, public interest law was a small, self-contained phenomenon, easily observed and easily measured. It has developed into a diffuse community of highly diverse organizations operating over a wide geographic and social map, posing many methodological challenges to those attempting to measure its size and scope. Even the organizational forms vary enormously: for example, a significant amount of public interest legal work takes place in the small but active contingent of private law firms—the "private public interest bar"—which provides representation to clients who cannot afford to pay the going rate for legal services. The survey findings discussed in this chapter, however, do not include private firm efforts, focusing instead on the crucial locus of public interest law activity: nonprofit public interest law centers.

As in the earlier surveys carried out in 1975 and 1979, public interest legal groups are defined as nonprofit, tax-exempt organizations, which employ at least one attorney and devote at least 30 percent of their total program effort to legal representation of otherwise unrepresented issues or constituencies on important questions of public policy. Approximately 15 percent are law school legal clinics. Business-oriented public policy law centers, such as the Pacific States Foundation and the Mid-America Legal Foundation, were excluded from this study, as explained in Chapter 4.

The Alliance mailed surveys to all known public interest legal organizations, requesting information on clients served, size of groups, types of activities, issues addressed, lawyers' salaries, and funding levels and sources. After a telephone follow-up effort, the Alliance received 158, or 71 percent, usable responses.[3] An additional thirty-eight organizations were identified as having disbanded or discontinued their legal programs since the 1975 survey. A stable core of 57 groups has existed throughout.

The Alliance, as in earlier surveys, divided public interest law centers into two major categories: client-defined and cause-defined. "Cause-defined" refers to civil rights/civil liberties (fifteen groups), environmental (twelve), media (seven), consumer (seven), international (three), and multi-issue (twenty-one) organizations. The "client-defined" category includes "minorities" organizations (eleven groups), serving blacks, Hispanics, Native Americans, or veterans; groups defending the rights of the poor (twenty-four), disabled persons (fifteen), women (fifteen), children (twelve), prisoners (six), lesbians and gay men (five), the elderly (three), or workers (two). Although the program classification of most organizations was obvious, some were less clear-cut, so a judgment was made as to the center's primary concern or client group. In addition, the lines between program types were blurred. For instance, although consumer groups spent the vast majority of their time on consumer issues, they also devoted some of their efforts to welfare and environmental concerns. In spite of such inescapable methodological difficulties, this system of classification shows the activities of public interest legal organizations as they have developed over time.

FINDINGS

Public interest law is a diverse field. Of the 158 centers surveyed, 41 percent were classified as "cause-defined" and 59 percent as "client-defined." (See Figure 2.1.) Multi-issue and civil rights/civil liberties

Figure 2.1
Distribution of Types of PILGs
(Number of Groups)

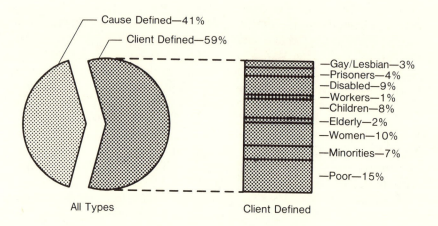

Cause Defined—41%

Client Defined—59%

—Gay/Lesbian—3%
—Prisoners—4%
—Disabled—9%
—Workers—1%
—Children—8%
—Elderly—2%
—Women—10%
—Minorities—7%
—Poor—15%

All Types   Client Defined

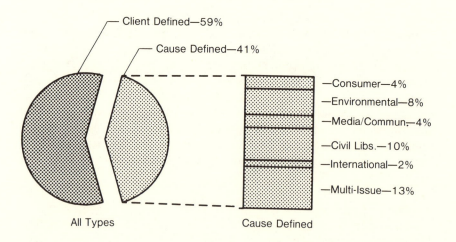

Client Defined—59%

Cause Defined—41%

—Consumer—4%
—Environmental—8%
—Media/Commun.—4%
—Civil Libs.—10%
—International—2%
—Multi-Issue—13%

All Types   Cause Defined

groups were the most numerous of the cause-defined type, accounting for 13 percent and 10 percent, respectively, of all organizations surveyed. Centers concentrating on environmental issues made up about 8 percent of the survey group. Among the client-defined groups, those serving the poor were the most numerous, accounting for about 15 percent of all centers surveyed. Groups serving the disabled constituted 9 percent; women, 10 percent; children, 8 percent; and prisoners, 4 percent.

The survey demonstrates that public interest legal centers are now more likely than in past years to focus on a specific issue or type of client. The multi-issue groups that exist tend to work on a few related areas. This trend toward a narrower range of issues is the result of several factors, including the desire on the part of funders to support specific projects rather than general programs and the increasing complexity of cases requiring greater specialization.

Growth Trends

Growth in the field of public interest law over the past two and a half decades has been dramatic. Figure 2.2 shows the overall increase in the number of centers from 1969 to the mid-1980s. Up to 1969, there were only twenty-three public interest law centers, staffed by fewer than fifty full-time attorneys. By the end of 1975, the number of centers had increased to 108, with almost 600 staff attorneys. In 1984, there were 158 groups employing a total of 906 lawyers.

The 1970s saw tremendous growth in the number of public interest legal organizations, with 111 groups established, an average of eleven per year. Since that time, the rate of growth has slowed considerably, with only nine new groups forming between 1980 and 1984.

Drawing information from the Alliance's two previous surveys, Figure 2.3 shows how the number of different types of organizations has changed over the years.

A number of factors contributed to the growth in numbers and variety of public interest legal centers in the seventies. During this period, many social movements seized on legal advocacy as a tool to assist citizens' groups and to further political causes. Between 1969 and 1975, the first groups serving consumers, minorities, the elderly, prisoners, workers, and gays and lesbians emerged. Since 1975, there has been an increase in the number of organizations concerned with protection of the disabled and with international human rights. The number of multi-issue groups such as the Center for Law and Social Policy (CLASP), the Center for Law in the Public Interest (CLIPI), and New York Lawyers for the Public Interest also grew during this period.

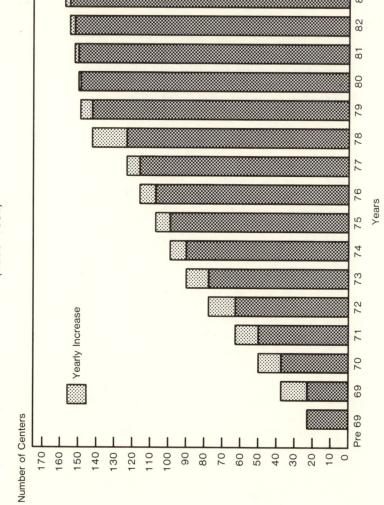

Figure 2.2
Growth Trends in Public Interest Law
(1969–1984)

Figure 2.3
Changes in Numbers of Different
Types of Organizations
(Client-Defined)

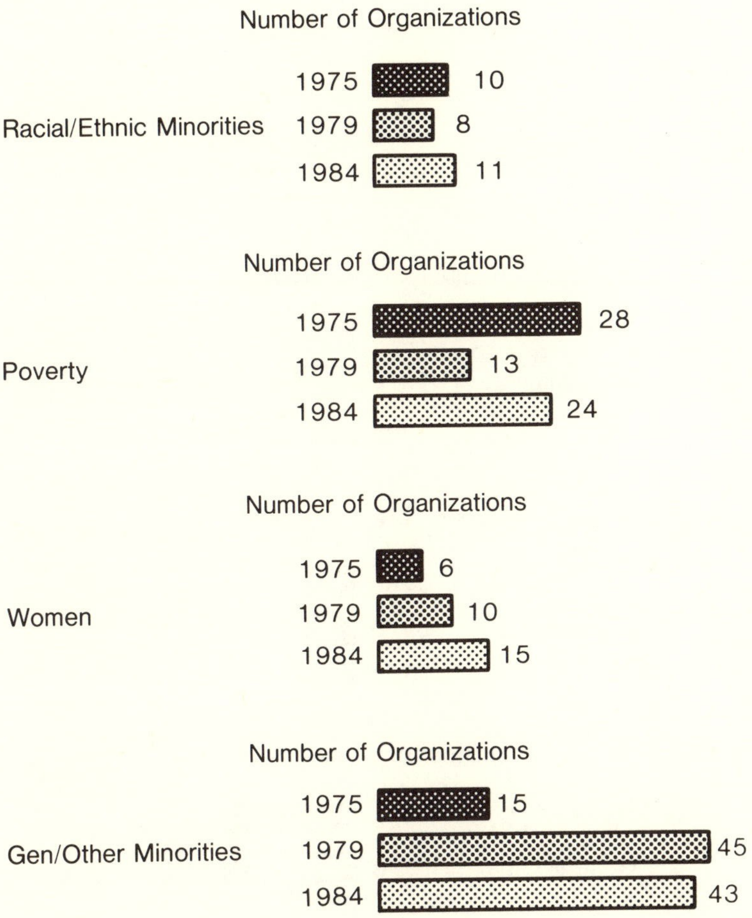

Number of Organizations

	1975	10
Racial/Ethnic Minorities	1979	8
	1984	11

Number of Organizations

	1975	28
Poverty	1979	13
	1984	24

Number of Organizations

	1975	6
Women	1979	10
	1984	15

Number of Organizations

	1975	15
Gen/Other Minorities	1979	45
	1984	43

(continued)

Figure 2.3 *(continued)*

Changes in Numbers of Different
Types of Organizations
(Cause-Defined)

Number of Organizations

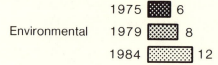

Civil Rights
Civil Liberties

1975 ▓ 3

1979 ▓▓▓▓ 11

1984 ▓▓▓▓▓ 15

Number of Organizations

Environmental

1975 ▓▓ 6

1979 ▓▓ 8

1984 ▓▓▓ 12

Number of Organizations

Consumer

1975 ▓▓ 7

1979 ▓ 6

1984 ▓ 7

Number of Organizations

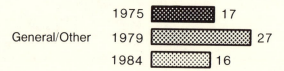

General/Other

1975 ▓▓▓▓▓▓ 17

1979 ▓▓▓▓▓▓▓▓▓ 27

1984 ▓▓▓▓▓ 16

Finally, many organizations which previously lacked a well-developed litigation component began to devote a significant portion of their work to legal advocacy. Examples of such groups include the Center for Science in the Public Interest, the American Council for the Blind, the Conservation Law Foundation of New England, the Reporters Committee for Freedom of the Press, and many Public Interest Research Groups (PIRGs). Indeed, in many areas of public policy, a growing recognition of the need for, and value of, legal advocacy has contributed to the measurable growth of activity seen in these surveys.

Geographic Location

Public interest law centers remained concentrated in the Northeast: 62 percent of the groups in the 1983–84 survey were headquartered there, almost the same proportion as reported in the 1975 survey. Twenty-three percent were located in the West, 8 percent in the Midwest, and 7 percent in the South. The cities with the most organizations were Washington, D.C. (forty-five groups), New York (thirty), San Francisco (thirteen), Los Angeles (nine), and Boston (nine). Still, about one-third of the centers, many of them working at the state or regional level, practiced outside these urban centers in locales as diverse as Eugene, Oregon; Walthill, Nebraska; Austin, Texas; and Gainesville, Florida. A significant change from 1975 was that the proportion of groups headquartered in Washington, D.C. fell from 44 percent to 29 percent. Since 1979, the number of public interest law centers in the Midwest and South remained about the same, while thirty-three new groups were identified in the Northeast and twelve in the West.

At the time of the most recent survey, representatives of all types of centers were found in the Northeast, including relatively large numbers of civil rights/civil liberties, women's, and multi-issue groups. Many anti-poverty, environmental, disability rights, and gay rights groups were headquartered in the West. About one-fourth of them had branch offices, and about half of these were in the Northeast, generally acting as legislative offices in Washington, D.C. Although the need for public interest advocacy is just as profound in the Midwest and South, many issue areas remain unaddressed in these regions. This is due in large part to what Nancy Davis of Equal Rights Advocates, a San Francisco-based group, calls "geographic discrimination" on the part of private foundations, which, she believes, "makes it harder for groups west of the Hudson to justify their work to funders."[4]

Activities

During 1983–84, most centers were engaged in a variety of activities which went beyond the traditional "test case" or class action litigation. About three-quarters supplemented their litigation with other forms of legal advocacy and legislative activities. Almost two-thirds represented or advised individuals, and an equal proportion engaged in community organizing or public education work.

About four-fifths of these organizations lobbied Congress and/or state legislatures, devoting an average of 10 percent of their efforts to such activities. This percentage has risen slightly since 1975, but since public interest legal organizations are tax-exempt under Section 501(c)(3) of the Internal Revenue Code, the amount of time they may devote to lobbying is limited by law.

Almost all groups were doing more community organizing. The amount of time spent working with local and regional constituencies doubled since 1979 from 5 to 10 percent.

Government Targets

Environmental, consumer, media, and international groups had a national focus, directing more than half of their efforts at Congress and the federal agencies. Multi-issue legal centers, in contrast, pursued much of their legal work at the state and local levels. The work of civil rights/civil liberties, poverty, women's rights, and disability groups was split almost evenly among the three levels of government. Children's rights groups focused mainly on local government, targeting about 26 percent of their efforts there, in contrast to an average of about 11 percent for the survey group as a whole.

Organizational Profiles

Budgets

The annual budget of those surveyed ranged from $16,000 to $10 million, with most organizations (64 percent) in the $100,000 to $999,999 range.

Only four groups, the American Civil Liberties Union (ACLU), the NAACP Legal Defense and Education Fund (NAACP/LDF), the Natural Resources Defense Council, and California Rural Legal Assistance, reported 1983 budgets of $4 million or more; the largest, the ACLU, had an annual budget of $10.7 million.[5] But even these relatively well-funded public interest law organizations were considerably smaller than the largest nonlegal nonprofits. The Urban League's 1982 budget, for example, was about $18 million, and that of the American Association of Retired Persons was $110 million.

Staffing Patterns

Staff Attorneys. The number of full-time public interest attorneys increased from less than fifty in 1969 to 600 in 1975, to 906 in 1984. But this increase was the result of the inclusion of new centers, not a sign that organizations were increasing in size. Indeed, the proportion of organizations with more than five full-time attorneys on staff shrank from 46 percent in 1975 to 28 percent in 1984. Thirty-eight percent had three to five lawyers and 33 percent employed one or two.

As Table 2.1 shows, poverty and civil rights firms employed the largest number of full-time attorneys. But these figures are distorted by the three or four centers in each category with legal staff of more than fifteen. The median figures more accurately reflect the staff size of the majority of civil rights and poverty groups. The median number of attorneys was four, again indicating that the large offices of such groups and the ACLU, the NAACP/LDF, and the Natural Resources Defense Council were the exceptions rather than the rule.

Table 2.2 compares the proportional share of lawyers employed by the various program types. Civil rights centers accounted for 10 percent of all organizations but employed 17 percent of all attorneys; poverty law firms, representing 15 percent of the survey group, employed 25 percent of the total number of lawyers. At the other end of the scale, women's law organizations constituted 8 percent of the total but employed only 4 percent of the attorneys.

Cooperating Attorneys. Much of the legal work of public interest organizations was not performed by the full-time staff attorneys, but rather by cooperating attorneys. Over three-fourths of the groups called upon outside counsel to handle some of their litigation, with more than half of these attorneys working on a voluntary basis.

Outside attorneys performed 28 percent, on average, of the legal work of surveyed groups, whose success depended to a great extent on the availability of these volunteers. Some organizations had well-developed programs to ensure a smooth working relationship between staff lawyers and volunteer and/or retained outside counsel. The Women's Legal Defense Fund, for example, retained approximately sixty volunteers in its Emergency Domestic Relations program and offered them periodic training sessions and a manual on defending battered spouses. Some of these attorneys worked for the government or corporations, while others were recent law school graduates seeking public interest experience.

TABLE 2.1   Staff Attorneys by Program Type: Total Number
and Median, 1983–84

Program Type	Number of Full-Time Attorneys	Median
Minorities	65	4
Poverty	228	6
Women	32	2
Children	36	3
Prisoners	20	5
Disabled	58	3
Gay/lesbian	5	1
Workers	10	5
Civil rights/civil liberties	157	4
Environmental	102	5
Consumer	19	3
International	7	1
Media	17	2
Multi-issue	122	6
ALL GROUPS*	906	4

*Three centers did not report the number of full-time attorneys employed.

SOURCE: Alliance for Justice survey of public interest legal organizations, 1983–84.

TABLE 2.2   Percentage of All Groups v. Percentage of All
             Lawyers Employed

Program Type	Percentage of All Groups	Percentage of All Lawyers Employed
Minorities	7%	7%
Poverty	15	25
Women	8	4
Children	7	4
Prisoners	4	3
Disabled	10	7
Gay/lesbian	3	1
Workers	1	1
Civil rights/civil liberties	10	17
Environmental	8	11
Consumer	5	2
International	2	1
Media	5	2
Multi-issue	13	13
	100%	100%

SOURCE: Alliance for Justice survey of public interest
legal organizations, 1983–84.

For several decades the NAACP/LDF has operated a cooperating attorney program which retains forty to sixty lawyers each year. These attorneys pursue civil rights cases in cooperation with the Fund, either as volunteers or as part of their private practice. Cooperating lawyers are brought together at a yearly conference to discuss current civil rights issues. In addition, NAACP/LDF's Capital Punishment Program augments its small staff with a network of well over a hundred volunteer attorneys handling cases on behalf of death row inmates. The Sierra Club Legal Defense Fund has approximately sixty lawyers in its outside counsel program.

Legal Interns. In addition to staff and outside attorneys, almost 1500 law students participated annually in internship programs, about twice the 1979 number. Some of these internships are in-house, while others are clinical legal education programs operated in cooperation with public interest firms. These interns continue to be an important legal resource for many organizations. Some, such as the Lawyers' Committee for Civil Rights Under Law, pay their interns a stipend during the summer.

Nonlegal Professionals. The survey identified a thousand other professionals—fundraisers, editors, managers, administrators—working for public interest legal centers. The proportion of these nonlegal professionals rose dramatically. In the 1975 and 1979 surveys, attorneys made up about 60 percent of all professional staff. In the 1983–84 survey, that proportion had dropped to 47 percent. This reduction may be attributed to a combination of factors: funding difficulties; a greater emphasis on nonlitigation strategies; and the increasing importance of administrative, fundraising, and membership development functions. The result is that organizations found it necessary to rely more on volunteer attorneys and legal interns, and less on full-time staff lawyers.

The same trend toward diversification of professional staff has been observed among other types of nonprofit service organizations as a result of federal budget cuts and intensified competition for philanthropic dollars. "You are seeing an increasing professionalization of charitable staffs," commented Lawrence Stinchcom, head of the Community Foundation of Greater Washington. "They [nonprofits] have to if they want to survive."[6]

Staff Attorneys: A Profile

The 1983–84 survey identified 906 full-time staff attorneys working for public interest legal organizations. About one-fifth were experienced lawyers who had been practicing twelve years or more. On the other hand, more than one-third had been at the bar for five years or less, and many were just entering the field.

In terms of years of experience, the majority of the attorneys in the survey had been practicing for three to five years. Civil rights attorneys had more experience than others, with about one-fourth out of law school for fifteen years or more, and over half out for nine years or more. Women's rights advocates were also more experienced, with the majority out of law school three to eight years, and one-quarter for

TABLE 2.3 Salary Distribution of Staff Attorneys,
1979 and 1983-84

Salary Level	1979	1983-84
Less than $10,000	2%	*
$10,000-$15,999	14	*
Less than $15,000	*	9
$16,000-$20,999	23	12
$21,000-$30,999	39	26
$31,000-$40,999	17	26
$41,000-$50,999	3	17
More than $50,999	2	*
$51,000-$60,999	*	6
More than $61,000	*	4

*Figures not available.

SOURCE: Alliance for Justice surveys of public interest law
centers, 1979 and 1983-84.

over eight years. Most environmental advocates have three to five years
of experience.

Public interest attorneys received comparatively modest salaries. Almost half earned $30,999 a year or less, and another one-fourth earned
between $31,000 and $40,999. Only one-tenth earn $50,000 or more.
(See Table 2.3). In dramatic contrast, a recent graduate starting out
in a large New York firm in 1984 could have expected to receive a
salary of $50,000.[7]

In the 1983 survey the salaries of a few staff attorneys climbed
above $61,000 a year for the first time and the proportion in the
highest salary ranges showed substantial gains. In 1983, 27 percent
earned more than $41,000, compared to only 5 percent in 1979.

As Table 2.4 indicates, there were substantial differences in typical
salary levels among different types of public interest legal organizations.

Civil rights and environmental lawyers earned higher than average
salaries. Forty-nine percent of the civil rights attorneys earned mid-

TABLE 2.4   Attorney Salary Ranges by Program Type, 1983-84

Program Type	Number and Percentage of Attorneys in Each Salary Range		
	LOW ($21,000)	MEDIUM ($21,000-$40,999)	HIGH ($41,000)
Minorities	7 (12%)	33 (55%)	20 (33%)
Poverty	64 (29%)	114 (53%)	39 (18%)
Women	3 (10%)	20 (67%)	7 (23%)
Children	7 (21%)	25 (73%)	2 (6%)
Elderly	1 (6%)	15 (83%)	2 (11%)
Prisoners	8 (27%)	16 (53%)	6 (20%)
Disabled	16 (29%)	35 (62%)	5 (9%)
Gay/lesbian	2 (40%)	3 (60%)	___
Workers	3 (30%)	7 (70%)	___
Civil rights/ civil liberties	14 (9%)	73 (49%)	63 (42%)
Environmental	14 (15%)	31 (33%)	48 (52%)
Consumer	10 (53%)	6 (31%)	3 (16%)
International	---	5 (71%)	2 (29%)
Media	2 (12%)	11 (65%)	4 (23%)
Multi-issue	36 (31%)	52 (45%)	27 (24%)
ALL GROUPS[*]	187 (22%)	446 (52%)	228 (26%)

[*]Nine groups did not provide attorney salaries.

SOURCE: Alliance for Justice survey of public interest legal organizations, 1983-84.

range salaries of between $21,000 and $40,999 a year, while 42 percent were in the high salary range, making $41,000 or more. Thirty-three percent of the environmental lawyers earned salaries in the middle range and 52 percent in the high range. One reason for these comparatively higher average salaries is that these areas are served by older, larger organizations. Further, many of their staff lawyers have been working for long periods of time, building their salary levels through seniority. Even these relatively high salaries, however, were much lower than those of lawyers with comparable experience in the private bar.

Disability rights advocates earned considerably less than the modest norms. Sixty-two percent were earning mid-range salaries in 1983–84, while 29 percent made less than $21,000. The salaries of consumer rights advocates were even lower, with 53 percent earning less than $21,000 and only 16 percent earning more than $50,000. Poverty attorneys also earned less than the norm: nearly one-third fell in the low salary range.

The salaries of lawyers working for women's legal groups were also comparatively low, with 10 percent making less than $10,000 a year and only 23 percent earning more than $50,000. Women's groups operate on a tighter shoestring, and consequently pay lower salaries than their civil rights counterparts.

Funding

Centers reported extremely diverse sources of funding. Compared with past years, the 1983–84 survey showed an increasing reliance on contributions from individuals (including both donations and membership fees) and a simultaneous decrease in the proportions supplied by the government and private foundations.

The financial support of individuals, through donations and member dues, was the largest single source of funding, accounting for 31 percent of all income. (Of this figure, 20 percent came from charitable contributions and 11 percent from membership dues.) Foundations grants were the second most important source of income, supplying 24 percent of total revenues, while the federal government supplied only 18 percent. Together, these three sources accounted for 73 percent of aggregate income. The remaining 27 percent was supplied by the following: court-awarded attorneys' fees (9 percent); corporate donations (3 percent); state and local government grants (3 percent); sales of materials (2 percent); Combined Federal Campaign contributions (1 percent); and income from a variety of sources such as interest on bank accounts, speaker fees, and luncheons and conferences (7 percent). Church contributions, funds from the private bar, lawyer trust fund accounts, and loans made up the remaining 2 percent of total income.

Figure 2.4 shows the proportions of these different sources of funding for a hypothetical average public interest legal center.

Foundation grants were the most widely distributed funding source, going to 81 percent of all surveyed organizations. About 35 percent received some revenues from the federal government, 74 percent from individual contributors, and 30 percent from membership dues.

The fact that individual contributors and members made up the most important single funding source for surveyed groups indicates that outreach efforts to the general public, mounted in the wake of government funding cuts, realized considerable success. Groups in many fields drew upon a large reservoir of public approval for their goals and activities and translated this positive public feeling into cash support through strategies such as direct mail appeals and membership drives.

The amount of government support for public interest law organizations was smaller than that for other nonprofits. According to estimates of the Urban Institute Nonprofit Sector Project, federal, state, and local government funds combined comprised an average 39 percent of the 1982 revenues of a wide range of nonprofit service organizations.[8] In contrast, the federal plus state/local contributions to public interest legal groups amounted to just 18 percent of overall revenues. Surveyed centers received only a fraction—$17.9 million in 1983—of all government dollars that flowed through nonprofits, a figure estimated at $32.3 billion dollars in 1980.[9] Indeed, more government dollars went to private law firms than to public interest law centers: federal government payments to private counsel totaled about $50 million each year,[10] and corporations continue to write off at least $1 billion in legal fees each year as business expenses.

Another difference between the funding base of public interest legal centers and other nonprofits remains that the latter obtain a large proportion of their income from fees charged for services: in 1981, they received 28 percent of their income from this source.[11] However, IRS regulations specifically forbid public interest legal centers to charge client fees.[12]

Although surveyed centers received 9 percent of their overall income from court-awarded fees, such revenue can only be realized through a favorable court judgment or settlement. They are therefore quite different from client fees, which are tied to services rendered and are more predictable. Consequently, public interest legal groups are at a financial disadvantage compared to other types of nonprofits.

Figure 2.4
Average PILGs
Reliance on Various Funding Sources

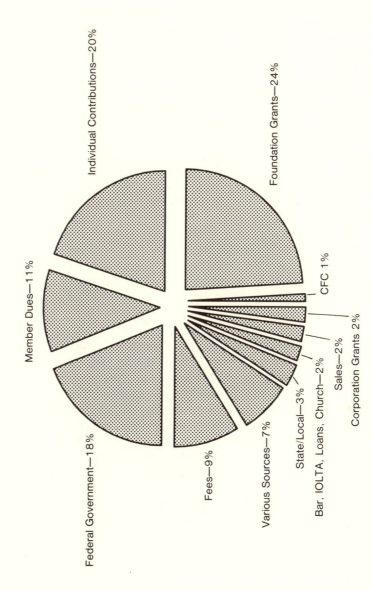

Individual Contributions—20%

Foundation Grants—24%

CFC 1%

Corporation Grants 2%

Sales—2%

Bar, IOLTA, Loans, Church—2%

State/Local—3%

Various Sources—7%

Fees—9%

Federal Government—18%

Member Dues—11%

These two factors—a relatively low reliance on government funding and the IRS ban on client fees—explain public interest law organizations' greater dependence on charitable contributions from individuals, foundations, and corporations. Nonetheless, they received a very small proportion of such contributions. Of the nearly $65 billion in total charitable giving in 1983,[13] public interest legal centers received $60 million, or slightly more than one-tenth of one percent.

Individual giving, the largest component of charitable contributions, exceeded $58 billion in 1983,[14] but individual contributions (including membership dues) to public interest legal organizations that year came to just $32 million, or about one-half of 1 percent of that total. Similarly, foundation grants to public interest law centers totaled $25 million, less than 1 percent of the $3.46 million in overall foundation giving that year.[15] The charitable giving of corporations was about $3 billion,[16] with only $2.7 million (about one-tenth of one percent), plus an additional $1.5 million of in-kind contributions, going to surveyed groups. Church giving to public interest law firms also made up only a minute fraction of overall contributions by religious institutions. Eighteen of the organizations in the survey received a combined total of approximately $650,000 in such funds, but church contributions to nonprofits were estimated at $8.5 billion in 1983.[17]

Distribution of Resources

In 1983–84, most of the resources in the field were concentrated in a few large organizations. Indeed, the 18 percent of surveyed groups with annual budgets of $1 million or more accounted for 67 percent of the total revenues of all legal centers. About two-thirds of the organizations were mid-sized, with annual budgets of between $100,000 and $999,999. These groups, however, accounted for only 32 percent of total revenues. The 18 percent of centers that were small (with budgets of less than $100,000) accounted for only 1 percent of the resources. Figure 2.5 shows the distribution of income among small, medium, and large organizations.

The larger centers are generally the older ones that have developed considerable public support and a stable and diversified funding base over the years. The most well-endowed organizations in the 1983–84 survey were, in descending order: the American Civil Liberties Union, the NAACP/LDF, the Natural Resources Defense Council, California Rural Legal Assistance, the Southern Poverty Law Center, the Children's Defense Fund, the Environmental Defense Fund, the Mexican American Legal Defense and Educational Fund, the Sierra Club Legal Defense Fund, the Native American Rights Fund, the Lawyers' Committee for

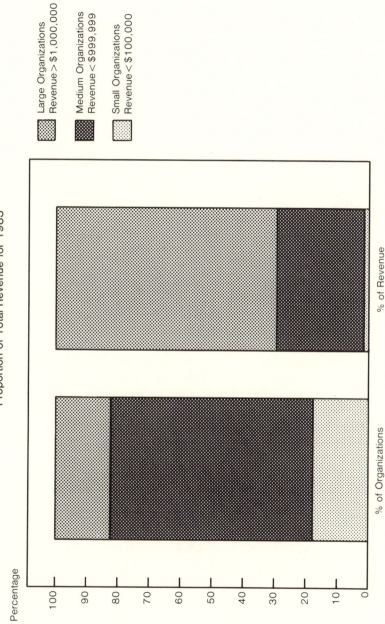

Figure 2.5
Number of Small, Medium and Large Organizations
Proportion of Total Revenue for 1983

Civil Rights Under Law (national office), and New York Public Interest Research Group (PIRG).

All of these groups had incomes in 1983 of more than $2 million. Furthermore, all of them except California Rural Legal Assistance, the Sierra Club Legal Defense Fund, and New York PIRG were ranked among the largest in the 1975 survey.

Distribution of Resources by Program Type

Civil rights/civil liberties groups and minority defense funds accounted for the largest share (30 percent) of the combined income of all public interest legal organizations. These were followed by poverty (19 percent), environmental (16 percent), and multi-issue (12 percent) groups. The remaining 23 percent of total resources were spread among all other program types. In terms of budget size, civil rights/civil liberties organizations also topped the list, averaging $2 million each. They were followed by environmental ($1.7 million) and poverty ($984,000) centers.

The share of funding accounted for by different program types changed over time, as Table 2.5 shows.

The share of overall funding decreased for poverty groups since 1975 from 28 percent to 19 percent, while the shares accounted for by environmental groups increased from 10 to 16 percent and by women's groups from 1 to 6 percent. Civil rights/civil liberties centers' amount of total revenues rose from 12 to 22 percent, while minority defense funds' share dropped from 24 to 8 percent.

Dependence on different funding sources varies widely by program type, as Table 2.6 shows.

Most groups had diverse funding bases. Support for environmental and civil rights/civil liberties centers, for example, came almost equally from private foundations, membership dues, and individual contributions. Most organizations received a significant amount of revenue from court-awarded attorneys' fees, and consumer groups received nearly one-third of their overall income from the sale of publications.

CONTINUING CONCERNS AND CONSTRAINTS

Although financial support for public interest law is still developing and growing, most program directors agree that funding is not nearly adequate to meet the needs of their constituencies, nor to afford them an equal opportunity to obtain justice in public forums such as the courts and administrative agencies. Almost all of the groups surveyed reported that lack of funding has limited their legal advocacy programs.

TABLE 2.5   Distribution of Resources by Program Type,
            1975, 1979, 1983

Client-defined Program Type	1975	1979	1983
Poverty	28%	13%	19%
Minorities	24	18	8
Women	1	2	6
General/other	14	24	14
(Children)	*	6	6
(Disabled)	*	6	4
(Prisoners)	*	3	2
(Workers, gay/ lesbian, elderly)	*	*	2
(Minority Defense Funds)	*	5	*
(Other)	*	4	*
TOTAL	67%	57%	47%

Cause-related Program Type	1975	1979	1983
Civil rights/ civil liberties	12%	10%	22%
Environmental	10	14	16
Consumer/other	9	15	13
(Multi-issue)	*	8	12
(Business-oriented)	*	7	*
(International/ media)	*	*	1
TOTAL	33%	43%	53%

* Figures not available

SOURCE: Alliance for Justice surveys of public interest
legal organizations, 1975, 1979, 1983-84.

TABLE 2.6   Funding Reliance by Selected Program Type, 1983

Program Type	Funding Sources[*]						
	Fdns.	Dues	Contribs.	Gov't.	Sales	Fees	Other
Minorities	39%	1%	11%	15%	1%	10%	23%
Poverty	8	14	--	59	2	4	13
Women	37	3	20	18	1	4	17
Children	57	--	3	14	4	6	16
Disabled	13	--	5	34	--	3	45
Civil rights/ civil liberties	23	24	25	1	--	15	12
Environmental	26	22	31	1	9	3	8
Consumer	15	28	12	--	31	--	14
Media	55	14	5	--	9	--	17
Multi-issue	17	11	31	3	--	15	23
ALL GROUPS	24	11	20	18	2	9	16

[*]Abbreviations

Fdns. = Private foundations
Dues = Membership dues
Contribs. = Individual contributions
Gov't. = Federal government
Sales = Sales of materials
Fees = Awards of attorneys' fees
Other = Revenue from churches, corporations, the private
bar, state and/or local governments, the Combined Federal
Campaign, Interest on Lawyers' Trust Accounts (IOLTA),
loans, honoraria, and/or special events.

SOURCE: Alliance for Justice survey of public interest
legal organizations, 1983-84.

The following examples typify the problems faced by public interest law groups today:

Being forced to close down programs or offices because of funding difficulties. There have been some casualties of the funding uncertainties of the 1980s. California Rural Legal Assistance was forced to shut down its Hollister, California office in 1984. The National Center for Youth Law eliminated one of its two offices and lost two attorneys due to funding cuts in 1982.[18]

Having to limit case volume to a fraction of the need for assistance. "We have an ocean of unmet need," writes the Indian Law Resources Center; "we are doing 1 to 2 percent of what we really need to be doing." The National Senior Citizens Law Center reports that "limited funding has curtailed the program's ability to take all the litigated cases at the request of local programs." The Women's Advocacy Project, an organization based in Austin, Texas, reports that "our funding is so limited that we can offer our services only four hours a day and hire two employees for just twenty hours per week."

Having to impose constraints on the kinds of cases taken according to their potential complexity and cost, on the types of legal strategies used, or on the types of clients served. "The problem is that the costs of successfully pursuing the kind of complex class actions that we bring has been rising faster than our income," writes the NAACP/ LDF. "We must be more careful than ever to evaluate each case which we investigate for its cost-effectiveness as well as its legal merit," agrees the Massachusetts Public Interest Research Group. The Center for Law in the Public Interest concurs: "It is extremely difficult to take on large administrative challenges (e.g., challenges to the licensing of nuclear power plants). We are extremely limited in the amount of technical assistance we can secure." The Public Interest Law Center of Philadelphia writes: "[We have] turned down participating in major Title VII class action[s] because [they are] beyond our resources. Numerous cases must be referred to others or turned down because of [a] shortage of personnel."

Staff cuts or high turnover rates because of work overload, organizational stress, or static, low salary levels. "Current personnel are grossly underpaid, given their expertise and ability," reports Equal Rights Advocates. "We will lose them if salaries are not increased . . . [We are] understaffed at all levels." "The funding situation," writes Advocates for Basic Legal Equality, "has caused reduction in staff and therefore, the acceptance of fewer cases. Because of financial uncertainties, it has made it difficult to recruit and retain high quality professionals. Many important projects are being held in abeyance."

Furthermore, because most foundations prefer to fund special projects rather than general operations, some centers are forced to relinquish talented lawyers when their projects terminate. "If there is not another project for them to work on, they must leave, and in any event an organization loses their expertise when they are moved into something new," writes New York Lawyers for the Public Interest.

Having to use attorney time for organizational functions such as fundraising, public relations, and administrative duties. Shortage of funds "has a dramatic effect," according to the Washington Lawyers' Committee, "diverting staff energy to fundraising from program work." In the two years following the Mental Health Law Project's loss of federal funds, Executive Director Norman Rosenberg spent 90 percent of his time in search of additional foundation funding for the group, thus further reducing its already reduced legal staff.[19]

Inability to carry out public education activities or to modernize equipment. The National Senior Citizens Law Center reports that the funding situation "has prevented us from maintaining the level of publication and dissemination of training materials we had previously maintained. It has prevented us from obtaining any word processing equipment."

Inability to plan for future growth and development. Funding uncertainties create a crisis mentality and make it impossible to plan for the long range, in terms of either specific programs or overall goals. The Lawyers' Committee for Civil Rights Under Law of the Boston Bar Association reports that its "project to combat racial violence desperately needs refunding. We are unable to project its future because of the unpredictability of foundations' providing grants." The Disability Rights Education and Defense Fund finds that "the impact is reduced ability to undertake long-term planning [and a] limited approach to case work and related activities."

The resilience that the public interest legal community has demonstrated in the face of funding difficulties should not be used as an excuse for complacency on the part of funders. Legal centers have experienced considerable erosion and dislocation of their funding base and have had to adjust to the less supportive political climate of the eighties. As a result, the foundation of public interest law in this country has been seriously shaken.

These groups have displayed resourcefulness, ingenuity, and dogged perseverance in recent years. But what has worked for them in the short term is unlikely to be sufficient in the future. If public interest law is to continue to play its crucial role, funders must become more aware of, and concerned with, legal advocacy issues and must take positive steps to foster and preserve public interest legal organizations.

Notes

1. Saint Ives, 13th century poverty lawyer and saint.

2. E. Warren, "Equal Justice Under Law," in *Law and Theology*, ed. A.J. Buehmer (St. Louis: Concordia, 1965).

3. The Alliance sent surveys to 282 groups. Excluding the sixty respondents which did not fit the definition of a public interest law firm, 158 usable questionnaires were returned.

4. Alliance interview with Nancy Davis, Executive Director, Equal Rights Advocates, February 7, 1984.

5. The survey included one center, the Women's Advocacy Project, founded in 1984. However, because all the other groups reported 1983 financial information, the Project's budget was calculated for that year as well.

6. Linda duBuclet, "Charities Alter Funding Strategy," *Washington Post*, (June 13, 1985), p. DC1.

7. "Trying to Keep Up With the Joneses," *The National Law Journal* 8, 21 (February 3, 1986), p. 2.

8. Lester M. Salamon, "The Results Are Coming In," *Foundation News* 25, 4 (July/August 1984), p. 18.

9. Lester M. Salamon and Alan Abramson, *The Federal Budget and the Nonprofit Sector.* (Washington, D.C.: Urban Institute Press, 1982), p. 48.

10. David Lauter, "US Paid $50 Million to Private Firms," *National Law Journal*, vol. 7, no. 14 (February 4, 1985), p. 51.

11. Salamon, "Results," p. 18.

12. See Chapter 1 for a consideration of the rationale for barring public interest legal organizations from charging client fees.

13. *Giving USA 1984 Annual Report* (New York: American Association of Fund-Raising Counsel, Inc., 1984), p. 7.

14. *Ibid.*

15. *Ibid.*

16. *Ibid.*

17. Jean A. McDonald, "Survey Finds Religious Groups Favor More Collaboration," *Foundation News* 23, 25 (September/October 1984), p. 21.

18. Unless otherwise noted, all information and quotations in this section are from the Alliance for Justice survey of public interest legal organizations, 1983–84.

19. Alliance for Justice interview with Lee Carty, Administrator, Mental Health Law Project, December 5, 1986.

3

Trends in Funding

Most of us recognize that the Right has much more money than we do, especially because of the generous infusion of corporate money beginning in the mid-1970s.[1]

The long-term trends in funding for public interest law give reason for cautious optimism. The overall funding picture showed a 51 percent increase in total resources between 1975 and 1983, from $70,107,500 to $105,588,110.[2] However, the increase in aggregate funding has not kept pace with the growth in the number of groups, from eighty-six in 1975 to 158 in 1983.[3] The budget of the average group in the 1983–84 survey was $776,383, a drop from the 1975 average of $815,203.

As Figure 3.1 shows, there was first a sharp decline and then an increase in funding for the average center. Between 1975 and 1979, the number of groups increased by 28 percent, while overall funding remained static, resulting in a decrease in the budget of the typical group. However, between 1979 and 1983, the increase in aggregate funding outpaced the growth in number of groups, and average group income increased 23 percent.

The overall rise in funding for public interest law was a tribute to the groups' resiliency and creativity in developing alternatives to make up for the lack of growth in traditional sources. The most dramatic change was in the amount supplied by sources other than the "big three" (foundations, government, and public contributions): alternative funding increased by a phenomenal 536 percent, from $2.8 million in 1975 to over $105 million in 1983. For the typical center, which experienced a decline in the amount of funding from traditional sources, the amount supplied by other sources increased from approximately $33,000 to over $200,000.

Many organizations anticipated that the Reagan Administration would try to cut back funding for public interest law and began diversifying their revenue bases early in this decade. Searching for ways to lessen

Figure 3.1
Funding Sources for Public Interest Law—1975, 1979, 1983
All Groups & Average Group

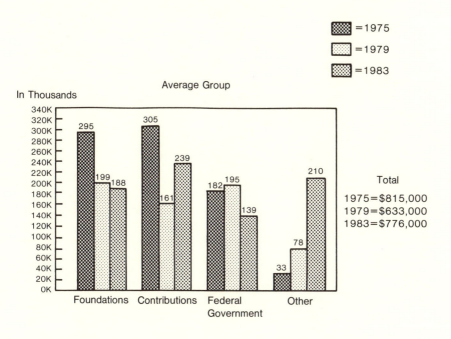

Average Group

In Thousands

Total

1975=$815,000
1979=$633,000
1983=$776,000

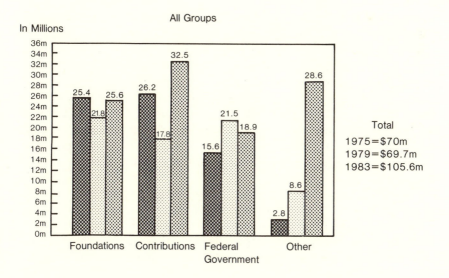

All Groups

In Millions

Total

1975=$70m
1979=$69.7m
1983=$105.6m

the reliance on traditional funders, they began exploring such strategies as workplace giving programs and sales of publications and other materials. However, though they have been crucial up to now, many of these new sources cannot be counted on for the future. Attorneys' fees, for example, which in 1983 were the largest single component of the "other" funding category, have become increasingly difficult to collect as efforts continue to overturn or circumvent the statutes mandating their provision. A broader concern, which will be more fully discussed in the next section, is that groups are now forced to devote so much of their time and resources to fundraising that their substantive program work is being hampered.

Foundation Support Declines

As Figure 3.1 shows, foundation support for public interest law remained constant between 1975 and 1983. However, because the number of groups increased by 58 percent during the same period, the average group actually experienced a 36 percent decline. Several factors explain the philanthropic community's failure to keep pace with growth in the field. First, a weaker economy in the seventies meant that existing foundations were forced to decrease the number and size of their grants. A recent study of philanthropy noted that "large foundations are not being established at the same rate as in the past."[4] This trend was accompanied, notes J. Craig Jenkins, a Professor of Sociology at the University of Missouri, by a sense of "pessimism about the possibility of solving social problems" which set in after the idealism of the sixties.[5]

Professor Jenkins also points out that the key role played by private foundations in the development of public interest law and other advocacy organizations in the early 1970s may have been an anomaly, since, generally, "foundation support goes overwhelmingly to conventional charitable activities and established institutions."[6] On the other hand, among the progressive foundations that continue to provide leadership on cutting-edge social issues there has been a trend to support newer concerns. The nuclear arms race, the Central American conflict, and other emerging issues are jostling aside the grant applications of traditional advocacy organizations in the funding marketplace.

Finally, in more recent years, some foundation executives have expressed a dislike for advocacy, and particularly litigation, as a strategy. They have joined with conservative critics of the judiciary who claim that American society has become too litigious, for which they hold public interest law groups at least partly responsible. This antipathy is heightened when, as sometimes occurs, the work of these groups conflicts with or even challenges the interests of foundation board members.

In spite of such changes, private foundations continue to be major supporters of public interest legal groups. Although the Ford Foundation began in 1979 to phase out funding to ten public interest law firms that it had helped establish in earlier years, it remained an important funder for organizations in the survey. Other large foundations frequently cited by surveyed centers included the Rockefeller, Carnegie, Edna McConnell Clark, Revson, Mary Reynolds Babcock, and Muskiwinni Foundations.

Government Funding Declines

With the election of Ronald Reagan in 1980, government funding for social and legal services was slashed. Both in aggregate and average-group terms, it rose slightly between 1975 and 1979 and then plummeted between 1979 and 1983, the aggregate by 12 percent and the average group by 29 percent. Thus, public interest legal organizations faced a substantial decline in government funding even as need and demand for their services were increasing.

Most centers, even those that received a substantial portion of their overall budget from the federal government, survived these cuts, but only by curtailing program services and reducing staff. The Women's Equity Action League (WEAL), for example, lost half of its $515,000 budget in 1981 but nonetheless ended 1982 with $482,000. Executive Director Char Mollison attributed the recovery to a reevaluation of the group's priorities undertaken in the wake of the cuts. "We assigned a dollar value to all of our services, and decided to cut back on the less essential ones." One result was that WEAL responded only to requests for information and assistance from its members, referring the general public to other organizations. The group targeted corporate donors for its annual fundraising dinner, with the result that these contributions made up 36 percent of WEAL's 1983 budget.[7]

The Mental Health Law Project, whose budget dropped from $850,000 in 1981 to $534,000 in 1983 as a result of federal cuts, responded by laying off three of its six staff attorneys and taking on less time-consuming cases. On the advice of a fundraising consultant, the Project began an intensive search for new foundation funding and developed a donor program; the latter provided about 14 percent of the group's total budget in 1986. Most importantly, believes Administrator Lee Carty, all of these changes were initiated early on, in some instances even before federal funding actually ended. Staff cuts, for example, were made in September 1980. The Project's current financial situation is proof of the effectiveness of such advance planning: it ended 1985 with a $790,000 budget.[8]

Public Contributions Increase

Public contributions underwent a "bust-and-boom" cycle between 1975 and 1983. Total donations dropped 32 percent between 1975 and 1979 and then rose a dramatic 83 percent between 1979 and 1983, actually topping the 1975 amount. However, 1983 contributions to the average center, while up from 1979, failed to match the 1975 level.

The 1975–79 drop is in part explained by the election of Jimmy Carter in 1976. During his administration, citizens' groups played an active role in government, helping to develop a strong record on environmental, consumer, and civil rights protection. Consequently, fewer people saw an immediate need to contribute to public interest law centers.

Ronald Reagan's election in 1980 all but closed the door to public participation in government, and it seems clear that the perception that advocacy groups were losing a substantial portion of their revenue at the exact time that their services were most needed was at least partly responsible for the resurgence of individual donations which began in 1980. It was also at this time that centers began making a special effort, through direct mailings, canvassing, and individual contacts, to build their membership and donor rosters.

Diversification of Funding Sources

The Alliance's 1983–84 survey of public interest law groups demonstrated that as federal and foundation funding declined over the years, centers significantly diversified their funding bases. The proportion provided by foundations and the federal government, which in past surveys were the two most important funding sources, dropped from 59 percent of overall income in 1975 to 42 percent in 1983. Correspondingly, the importance of other funding components grew. Income from court-awarded attorneys' fees, state and local governments, corporations, sales of publications, the Combined Federal Campaign and other workplace fundraising drives, and various other funding sources increased from 4 percent of overall funding in 1975 to 27 percent in 1983.

It is important to keep in mind, however, that all these sources of alternative funding represented small components of the overall picture for most organizations. Even dramatic growth in any single source, such as sales of publications or corporate contributions, did not fully compensate for the substantial cuts in foundation and government support in most cases.

Emerging Sources of Funding:
A Closer Look

This section examines some promising fundraising trends and strategies, including: the continuing struggle to realize court-awarded attorneys' fees; a new set of nationally based alternative foundations; the emergence of a variety of funders, both public and private, at the state and local levels; the efforts by a wide range of advocacy groups to gain access to the Combined Federal Campaign and other workplace giving drives; attempts to increase revenues from corporations through cash grants and in-kind contributions; experimentation with direct mail solicitation; increased efforts to raise revenues through the sale of publications and other materials; and the establishment of public interest legal foundations. (See Figure 4, Chapter 2 for a breakdown of this funding category.)

Court-awarded Attorneys' Fees

The general rule in American courts is that each party must bear the costs of its own legal fees. The most significant exception to this rule allows litigants to collect their attorneys' fees against their opponents in cases deemed to be in the public interest. Congress has enacted more than 150 statutes that provide fees to prevailing parties in civil rights, environmental, and consumer cases.

One of the most significant findings of the survey was that attorneys' fees awarded by the courts to prevailing parties in public interest cases provided a substantial amount of income for public interest legal centers. In the 1983–84 survey, ninety-eight groups reported applying for awards, and sixty-seven actually collected fees, most of them computed at market rate, totaling over $9.2 million. This represented a 200 percent increase over the $3 million collected in 1979.

Nearly half of all attorneys' fee awards in the 1983–84 survey went to civil rights and minority defense organizations, a higher proportion than in 1979. Poverty groups received almost 10 percent of the total, ten times more than they did in 1979. Senior citizens' and children's advocates also won more fee awards.

As the figures above indicate, the impact of the attorneys' fees statutes has been enormous. They have made it possible for thousands of citizens to obtain legal representation. They have also compensated public interest and private attorneys for their time and efforts in handling impact litigation. Nonetheless, they are not a dependable source of income. The Reagan Administration repeatedly sought the introduction of legislation which would substantially limit fees. While no such bill has passed, debate in Congress has focused on the costs rather than the benefits of fee awards. This hostile attitude has also manifested itself in the federal courts, where judges have applied the statutes narrowly in many cases and have been parsimonious in amounts awarded. Even when fees are awarded, they may come to the organization long after the case has been prepared and argued, a delay which often creates serious cash flow difficulties. The problem is particularly acute for new centers and private practitioners, who have even fewer cash reserves on which to depend while waiting to receive awards.

One lawyer who first represented the government and then plaintiffs in civil rights cases contrasted his experiences in collecting fees:

> When the government hires . . . [a] lawyer, he gets paid for all the time he spends, because the government is not looking at his timesheets and saying his time was excessive, redundant or unnecessary, or out of line with the importance of the government's goals. That lawyer . . . gets paid for all his time even if he loses the case, and he gets paid as the case goes along, every month. He has no trouble paying the rent and paying his staff when the bills fall due. That . . . lawyer is in a pretty secure position. I *know* how good that feels, because I once represented the City of Greenville, Mississippi in a civil rights case.
>
> What happens . . . to the . . . lawyer who is prosecuting a civil rights case? . . . I bring a voting rights case against a city in Mississippi and manage to have the City Council reapportioned. For the first time in recent memory, the council will be elected in a constitutional manner . . . I submit a petition for $75 an hour for the time I have put in. I have a court breathing down my neck, telling me in hindsight that I spent too much time in light of "minimal" results, because the court did not accept all of my contentions. Because the court failed to move three of seven district lines, it reduces my time by three-sevenths to reflect lack of success on particular issues. The court also deducts the time I spent on constitutional issues which it didn't decide because the case was decided on statutory grounds . . . The same high-priced lawyers who billed the taxpayer for all the time they spent, telling the court how weak my case was, now try to cut my fee by telling the court that my winning the case was not great shakes because it was a sure winner from the beginning. In the end, I recover for one-half of the hours I put in.[9]

Alternative Foundations

In the wake of reductions in funding for public interest law on the part of major foundations, a new group of foundations, some of them headed by the children and grandchildren of the country's philanthropic and corporate giants, emerged. Schooled in the civil and women's rights protests of the sixties, these young donors formed more than seventy foundations in order to support socially progressive organizations. Fourteen of these foundations form the New York-based Funding Exchange, an umbrella association of community funds which supports projects having "little or no access to traditional funding sources."[10] One member is the Haymarket People's Fund in Boston. In 1983 Haymarket made 155 grants totalling $276,431 to groups working for, among other things, community empowerment, gay and lesbian rights, and workplace democracy. The Fund for Southern Communities supports organizations in North and South Carolina and Georgia on issues such as civil rights and civil liberties, the rights of the poor, and alternative arts and media. The Fund made thirty-six grants ranging from $750 to $3,000 in 1983.[11]

As these figures suggest, most alternative funds have small endowments and are unable to make large, sustaining grants. However, many in the philanthropic community maintain that their influence is greater than the $3 billion they distribute annually[12] would suggest. They finance groups that are too controversial for traditional foundations, have organized a number of young, wealthy activists to make large contributions during their lifetimes, and generally serve as the "progressive conscience" for more mainstream members of the foundation establishment. The recently formed Network of National Grantmakers, which is comprised of many of the alternative funds, alerts the philanthropic community to emerging social issues.

The extent to which alternative foundations will support public interest legal groups is not clear. On one hand, many of the funders are themselves activists, and often work with traditional advocacy groups—women's, minorities, gay and lesbian, and prisoners' rights organizations—in the community. On the other hand, these funders in general prefer to support small, local centers and emerging or controversial issues.

Local and Regional Funders

Another developing funding pattern that has helped in a limited way to offset the loss of federal government and national foundation support is the emergence of local and regional funders interested in public interest law. There are currently 300 community foundations nationwide, thirty-five of which have formed since 1978, with assets totaling $3 billion.[13] These new funders are often private, regionally based foundations or groups of small alternative grantors that fund local legal advocacy.

In New York, for example, funders such as the Greater New York Fund, the New York Community Trust, and the New York Foundation have supported Advocates for Children of New York. Many Philadelphia area foundations, including the Community Trust of Philadelphia and the Philadelphia Foundation, have been quite responsive to the needs of local public interest legal centers. The Permanent Charity Fund of Boston and the Common Capitol Fund of Washington, D.C. have also been active in funding public interest law activities in their respective cities.

In addition, twenty-three centers reported receiving a total of $3.6 million in grants from state and local governments. Of the twenty-three, seven were multi-issue groups, six were disability rights, and five were children's groups. This amount constituted only a small proportion (about 3 percent) of total funding for public interest law organizations. What little state and local monies are disbursed most often go to legal service programs, according to Richard Shapiro, Director of the Public Interest Advocacy Division of the New Jersey Department of the Public Advocate, a state-financed office with an unlimited mandate to bring public interest litigation.[14]

Other states have been reluctant to fund advocacy units like the decade-old New Jersey Department. This government-sponsored public interest law firm has helped to fill the gap left when private advocacy groups were forced to cut back their services, but New Jersey remains the only state with such a program.

The Combined Federal Campaign and Other Workplace Giving Drives

In the early 1980s, public interest legal centers, along with other advocacy groups, mounted a successful effort to gain access to the Combined Federal Campaign (CFC), the annual workplace fundraising drive for federal government employees. The effort paid off: in 1983, these groups collected over $1 million. The Reagan Administration tried several times to exclude advocacy organizations from participating, claiming that the campaign ought only to support local health and direct services programs. In 1987, Congress enacted legislation guaranteeing eligibility to a wide range of charities, including advocacy groups.

A federation of nine legal and nonlegal women's groups raised close to $200,000 in 1985 by soliciting employees at the workplace. "As a coalition, we have the power to raise much more money than we could on our own," states Vicki Krama, a founding member of Women's Way.[15] The Women's Funding Alliance in Seattle raised nearly $40,000 in the same year, only its second year of workplace solicitation.[16]

Environmental groups in California also formed a coalition that carries out annual fundraising drives among state employees. Established by Earl Blauner of the Sierra Club Legal Defense Fund, the Environmental Federation raised $159,600 for fourteen environmental organizations in 1986.[17]

Corporate Grants and In-kind Contributions

Law centers have begun to tap into corporate philanthropic sources, although only in a small way. In 1983–84, thirty-six groups reported receiving corporate contributions totaling $2.7 million. More than half of these funds went to civil rights and minority defense groups, while women's and children's groups shared nearly one-third. The remainder was distributed among poverty, disability, media, multi-issue, and environmental groups.

About one-third of surveyed organizations also reported receiving in-kind corporate donations. *Pro bono* work by attorneys at private firms, which the public interest legal community has long relied on, was the most frequently mentioned, followed by donations of office space, furniture, and equipment; access to photocopiers and word processors; and professional or administrative assistance in areas such as fundraising and accounting. The twenty-six centers which reported the cash value of their gifts received almost $1.5 million of in-kind contributions.[18]

Direct Mail Solicitation

In recent years, the use of mass mailings to appeal for contributions and memberships from individuals has grown in popularity among public interest law organizations. Frances Dubrowski, formerly senior staff lawyer at Natural Resources Defense Council, reports that direct mail has yielded not only monetary returns but a growing "support base of thousands of new advocates who know the issues."[19] In 1983, sixty-five groups used direct mail for fundraising and membership development. Most environmental groups employ this strategy, as well as at least half of the civil rights, minority defense, and children's rights centers. Several women's, poverty, and multi-issue groups also reported undertaking such campaigns.

Organizations most likely to make these campaigns work for them already enjoy high name recognition and have sufficient financial and personnel resources to carry them out. Mass mailings necessitate substantial initial expense for printing, postage, and the development or purchase of mailing lists. It is often two to three years before the group establishes a large enough base of regular, active donors to make a return on its initial investment. Clearly, direct mail is no fundraising panacea for public interest law.

Pooling Resources

Many organizations have responded to the financial pinch of the 1980s by pooling resources in an effort to economize. In the 1983–84 survey, seventy-seven groups reported engaging in such cooperative efforts. They shared office space and equipment, undertook joint projects, legal and nonlegal, and raised funds together. In a 1984 effort spearheaded by the NAACP/LDF, several public interest and civil rights organizations in New York City joined together to share office space in a "public interest building." More recently, Consumers Union, the Migrant Legal Action Program, the Center for Auto Safety, the public interest law firm of Harmon and Weiss, and others created the Joint Support Center, a shared-space building in Washington, D.C.

Sales of Publications and Other Materials

Some public interest legal organizations have received a significant portion of their revenues from sales of publications and educational materials. The National Wildlife Federation, for example, raises nearly half of its operating budget from magazine subscriptions, including its popular *Ranger Rick* for children, and sales of other materials. The litigation office of Consumers Union is almost entirely funded by the proceeds from sales of *Consumer Reports*. The Center for Science in the Public Interest (CSPI) increased its budget from $390,000 in 1979 to $2,175,000 in 1985, mostly by revamping its *Nutrition Action* newsletter to appeal to the average consumer. In 1985, newsletter subscriptions accounted for more than 65 percent of CSPI's total budget, and sales of books and posters added another 20 percent.[20]

However, just as direct mail solicitation is not effective for every group, so also the sale of publications has limitations as a fundraising technique. In marketing *Nutrition Action*, CSPI was able to tap into an already strong interest in health and nutrition issues on the part of the general public. But groups which represent less popular issues will obviously have greater difficulty in selling publications on a large-scale, highly profitable basis.

Public Interest Legal Foundations

Another growing source of funding for public interest law is the public interest legal foundations (PILFs) and student-funded fellowships sponsored by many law schools and alumni organizations. About twenty-three law schools sponsor PILFs, which work cooperatively with the school and alumni groups to make grants to local public interest law centers and to provide funding for law students who want to work with these centers during the summer or after graduation.

PILFs have recently begun to diversify their funding sources, supplementing the traditional donations from law students and alumni with contributions from private law firms that recruit on campus; income from lectures, luncheons, and other special events; phone-a-thons aimed at older alumni; and matching grants from law firms, local foundations, and bar associations.

Some PILFs sponsor public interest internships and loan forgiveness programs to assist law school graduates who enter the low-paying public interest or legal services fields. PILFs inform law students about opportunities to practice public interest law and promote educational changes that integrate social justice and social change concerns into the legal curriculum.

About two dozen other law schools have similar mechanisms which, although they are not formally organized as PILFs, provide small grants, fund internship programs at local public interest law firms, or sponsor loan forgiveness programs.

Notes

1. David M. Gordon, "Up from the Ashes—III: Where's the Money Coming From?" *The Nation*, vol. 24, no. 7 (February 23, 1985), p. 206.

2. Unless otherwise noted, all figures in this section are in current 1983 dollars. Inflation rates, based on the GNP implicit price deflators presented in the *Economic Report of the President 1986*, were calculated at 32 percent for 1979–1983 and at 75 percent for 1975–1983.

3. Financial information was provided by 136 groups in the 1983–84 survey.

4. Teresa Odendahl, ed., *America's Wealthy and the Future of Foundations.* (New York: The Foundation Center, 1987), p. 2.

5. Craig Jenkins, "Foundation Funding of Progressive Social Movements," in *Grant Seekers Guide*, Jill R. Shellow, ed. (Mt. Kisco, New York: Moyer Bell Limited, 1985), p. 11.

6. *Ibid.*, p. 8.

7. Alliance for Justice interview with Char Mollison, Executive Director, Women's Equity Action League, December 5, 1986.

8. Alliance for Justice interview with Lee Carty, Administrator, Mental Health Law Project, December 5, 1986.

9. Statement of Charles T. McTeer, Hearing on S.2802 before the Subcommittee on the Constitution of the Senate Committee on the Judiciary, 98th Congress, second session, 379–81, 388 (1984).

10. Shellow, *Grant Seekers Guide*, p. 168.

11. *Ibid.*, p. 326.

12. Elsa Walsh, "Alternative Foundations Support Social Change," *Washington Post* (December 25, 1984), p. A1.

13. "Strengthening Local Philanthropy," *The Ford Foundation Letter*, vol. 18, no. 1 (February 1987), p. 1.

14. Alliance for Justice interview with Richard Shapiro, Director, Public Interest Advocacy Division, New Jersey Department of the Public Advocate, December 5, 1986.

15. "Women's Funds." A special report by the National Committee for Responsive Philanthropy (Washington, D.C.: National Committee for Responsive Philanthropy, July 1986), p. 4.

16. *Ibid.*, p. 5.

17. Alliance for Justice interview with Michelle Miller, Assistant to the Director, Environmental Federation, May 1, 1987.

18. For more information on in-kind corporate donations, see Alex J. Plineo and Joanne Scanlon, *Resource Raising: The Role of Non-Cash Assistance in Corporate Philanthropy* (Washington, D.C.: Independent Sector, 1986).

19. Alliance for Justice interview with Frances Dubrowski, senior staff lawyer at Natural Resources Defense Council, February 12, 1985.

20. Mary Searcy, "Marketing the Public Interest," *Pipeline*, a publication of the Alliance for Justice, no. 9 (Spring 1986), pp. 1, 6.

4

A Closer Look at the Practice
of Public Interest Law

You may, by observing the congestion of lawyers representing substantial corporate and individual financial interests, catch a glimmer of what the legal services situation must be for those whose economic situation often prevents them from retaining even the most meager legal assistance. This group consists not only of those in the South Bronx who are unable to fight their landlord or obtain the help needed to incorporate a small business, but also those who lie neglected in mental institutions and nursing homes . . . or who populate death row in our nation's prisons.[1]

Pacific Legal Foundation is a public interest law firm in the same way catsup [was] a vegetable under Reagan's . . . school lunch guidelines.[2]

This chapter examines first the various types of centers that make up the universe of traditional public interest law and participated in the Alliance for Justice's 1983–84 survey. The unique features of each major program type are discussed. Not every center in each category is mentioned; for a list of all the organizations identified by the Alliance in its survey, see Appendix B. Then, other types of practices are considered: conservative legal centers, private public interest firms, and the role of the private bar in public interest representation.

TRADITIONAL CENTERS

Centers for Civil Rights/Civil Liberties
and Racial and Ethnic Minorities[3]

Working to ensure minority groups' participation in the formulation of public policy, civil rights/civil liberties and minority defense organizations are the most firmly established, largest, and best endowed of all public interest organizations. They also employ more attorneys than any other program type, a total of 222.

The NAACP Legal Defense and Education Fund (NAACP/LDF), the American Civil Liberties Union (ACLU), and the Lawyers' Committee for Civil Rights Under Law are among the oldest public interest groups in the country, and have served as models for most of their successors. Over the years, centers such as the Native American Rights Fund (NARF), the Mexican American Legal Defense and Educational Fund (MALDEF), and the Asian American Law Caucus have formed to represent the interests of particular minority populations. The work of these groups is supplemented by networks of cooperating attorneys; in fact, an average of 37 percent of their litigation is handled by outside lawyers on a *pro bono* basis.

The civil rights centers developed the three basic organizational models after which most public interest groups are patterned. Many, like the Housing Advocates in Cleveland, Ohio, resemble private law firms, except that they depend on funding from outside sources. Others, such as the League of Women Voters Education Fund, are affiliated with a parent organization. Although they receive separate gifts and grants, they rely primarily on the parent group for funding and direction. Finally, groups such as NAACP/LDF are organized around a central office with a full-time staff and a network of cooperating lawyers. Another presence in the field is the recently established Legal Defense Fund of People for the American Way.

NAACP/LDF, with an annual budget of $6.9 million, is traditionally recognized as the legal arm of the civil rights movement. Founded in 1930, it pioneered the concept of public interest law; indeed, the term "legal defense fund" is today commonly used to describe civil rights advocacy organizations in general. NAACP/LDF has won hundreds of civil rights cases, including the 1954 landmark Supreme Court decision in *Brown v. Board of Education* which outlawed legally enforced segregation in public schools.

The combined annual budgets of the twenty-six groups in these two categories comprise 30 percent of the total funding for public interest law. Most of their support comes from public contributions (38 percent) and foundations (27 percent). Another important source is attorneys' fees, which accounted for 14 percent of their overall funding in 1983. Many of the older civil rights organizations—NAACP/LDF, the ACLU, the Lawyers' Committee—have built solid membership and individual donor bases which provide stable funding. The only centers to receive significant amounts of federal support were the Florida Justice Institute, the Native American Rights Fund (from the Legal Services Corporation), and Vietnam Veterans of America Legal Services.

The overall stability of civil rights organizations is demonstrated by the doubling of overall financial support for the category since 1979.

However, as a Ford Foundation report recently pointed out, a large share of that money is project-specific. They, like most other groups, have had difficulty securing core funding for their programs, and their ability to apportion resources effectively and engage in long-term planning has been hampered.[4]

Poverty Law Programs

The twenty-four centers that defend the rights of the poor comprise the second largest category of groups. Seventeen are special support or backup centers that provide legal and technical assistance to the more than 1,200 legal services offices across the country. Support center activities include consultations with and training of legal services attorneys, representation of eligible clients, and dissemination of information. Poverty groups work in such areas as housing, health, social security, welfare, and family law.

Over the past several years, poverty organizations have been engaged in a struggle for their own survival. At the same time, they have continued to meet an ever greater need for assistance from the Legal Services Corporation's (LSC) field attorneys. Burton Fretz, Executive Director of the National Senior Citizens Law Center, reported that between 1982 and 1984, requests for technical assistance from the Center doubled, from 2000 to 4000. He attributes this to an increase in the number of elderly poor and to the Social Security Administration's reluctance to award benefits. An added frustration is having to "represent clients with one's hand [tied] behind one's back" because of restrictions imposed by the LSC on the types of advocacy that legal services lawyers may undertake.[5]

In contrast with the 1970s, when seven new backup groups were formed, the first half of this decade witnessed the establishment of only one, a center for medically dependent children in Indianapolis. The slow rate of growth is primarily the result of cutbacks in federal support. In 1981, the overall budget for the LSC was $321 million. In 1986, it dropped to $292 million, then rose slightly to $305 million in 1987. The $7 million allocated for support centers in 1981 has not increased since then. Clearly, the decline in funding for legal services in recent years has been dramatic, particularly when the figures are adjusted for inflation.

While many of the support centers have been able to raise money from private sources, it has not been enough to make up for the loss of federal funds. Despite this, the backup centers have been credited by the offices they serve, as well as by many members of Congress, with maintaining a very high level of effectiveness.[6] One reason for this strong record is that the lawyers working for these groups have considerable experience. Directors have been practicing for an average of eighteen years, twelve of them within legal services. In eleven of the centers, the average attorney has more than ten years of experience.

There are also a few privately funded poverty law centers, which tend to work on a broader range of issues. The Montgomery, Alabama-based Southern Poverty Law Center, for instance, ranks among the largest and best funded public interest law centers. It has raised substantial amounts in public contributions through its direct mail campaign, one of the most successful in the country. In recent years, the Center has turned away from traditional civil rights cases in favor of combating white supremacy groups and anti-abortion organizations that use violence against abortion clinics.

Public Advocates, Inc., founded in 1971 in San Francisco, has brought more than 100 class action suits and has represented more than seventy organizations, including the Gray Panthers, the League of United Latin American Citizens, and the NAACP. In recent years, Public Advocates has turned to "more direct, political ways to reform and enforce the laws for their clients."[7]

Food Research and Action Center (FRAC) is an anti-hunger advocacy organization devoted to educating the poor about nutrition and ensuring that they are given a voice in food program policy decisions. FRAC counts among its many successes blowing the whistle on the Department of Agriculture's "catsup as a vegetable" rule and bringing about its withdrawal. This program would have considered condiments such as catsup and relish to be acceptable substitutes for vegetables in school lunch programs.[8]

Women's Law Centers

There have been substantial gains in the growth of and funding for women's legal groups. Since the early seventies, the number of centers has grown from five to fifteen, although the number of full-time attorneys employed has remained low, at an average of 2.5 per group.[9] Furthermore, their salaries are considerably lower than those of their colleagues: only 23 percent earn $41,000 or more, compared to 42 percent of the attorneys working for other civil rights organizations.

The newest groups are the Women's Advocacy Project in Austin, Texas and the Women and the Law Project, a clinical program of American University's Washington College of Law. Both were established in 1984. Other centers included for the first time in the 1983–84 survey are the National Women's Law Center, which in 1981 split off from the Center for Law and Social Policy, and the National Center for Women and Family Law, incorporated in 1979.

Overall funding for women's centers nearly doubled between 1975 and 1979, and quadrupled between 1979 and 1983. Accompanying this dramatic rise was a corresponding increase in the influence and national prominence of these groups. Nonetheless, their financial situation remains poor in comparison with other types of centers: women's groups represent 10 percent of the surveyed groups but account for only 6 percent of total funding.

Foundations appear to have responded to the outcry in the late 1970s for greater support for feminist causes. A 1979 Ford Foundation study on funding for women's issues reported that less than 1 percent of private foundation funding went to projects fighting sex-based discrimination or promoting opportunities for women in non-traditional fields; of that amount, only 14 percent went to groups engaged in "legal, political or community action."[10] The study found that a small group of foundations—Ford, Rockefeller, Carnegie, Mellon—were contributing the bulk of the funding for women's issues, and that most of the grants were made to a few prominent organizations and universities in the Northeast.[11]

These foundations continue to support women's issues, and they have been joined by eight new ones, including the MS, Windom, and Los Angeles Women's Foundations, which were specifically established to fund women's organizations.

Even though foundation funding has increased, women's centers have worked to diversify their funding bases. In 1975, more than 90 percent of the support for women's legal groups came from foundations. By 1983, this figure had dropped to just 37 percent as groups mounted aggressive fundraising campaigns to tap new sources of money. In 1983, for example, the National Organization for Women's Legal Defense and Education Fund (NOW LDEF) succeeded in matching the amount it received from foundations with contributions from corporations and individuals. Other groups have also collected substantial sums from fundraising events, corporate sources, awards of legal fees, and the Combined Federal Campaign.

Abortion rights and employment continue to dominate the dockets of most women's legal groups. The 1973 Supreme Court decision in *Roe v. Wade* recognizing a woman's constitutional right to an abortion did not close the book on the issue, and feminist lawyers continue to file numerous lawsuits to prevent the ruling from being eroded. In the face of the increasing "feminization of poverty," they also continue to work for economic equity. Advocates for women's rights are using existing federal and state antidiscrimination laws to increase educational opportunities for women, obtain equal pay for equal or comparable work, strike down pregnancy-based discrimination, and reform laws governing domestic relations.

Other Disadvantaged Populations

Children's Rights Centers

The number of groups advocating on behalf of children has also increased rapidly, from two in 1975 to twelve in 1983. The largest of these organizations, the Children's Defense Fund (CDF), has an annual budget of $6 million, a staff of sixty-seven (ten of whom are lawyers) and six branch offices in Minnesota, Mississippi, Ohio, Texas, New York, and Virginia. Others include the National Center for Youth Law in California and locally-focused centers such as the Education Law Center and the Juvenile Law Center, both in Philadelphia.

Until the beginning of this decade, government funding was a significant source of income for children's rights groups (except for CDF, which has never received federal support). Consequently, they were particularly hard hit by Reagan Administration cutbacks in funding for the Legal Services Corporation, Health and Human Services, and other federal departments. Federal grants and contracts for children's advocacy centers fell from $1.76 million in 1979 to $977,000 in 1983, a 44 percent drop even before inflation. This meant that the share of total federal funding for children's groups fell from more than half (54 percent) to less than a seventh (14 percent). Most of the centers were successful in offsetting these losses by raising funds from national and local foundations.

Children's advocacy organizations address a broad range of issues. Most state and local groups devote half of their time to education issues, pushing for the improvement of programs for handicapped children and working to strengthen the capacity of schools to respond to the needs of disadvantaged youths. Other areas covered include health, child care, adolescent pregnancy, foster care, and juvenile justice.

National children's groups have made a concerted effort to expand their work at the state level as resources have shifted from the federal to the state goverments and to handle increased requests for assistance from local client groups. CDF's six regional offices, for example, were established to work on projects at the local level. Legal centers in New York and Philadelphia have also stepped up their efforts to secure more state and local funding for children's programs. In 1984, the Association of Child Advocates was formed to coordinate state-based children's groups at a national level.

Prisoners' Rights Centers

The number of legal organizations defending the rights of prisoners has increased from two in 1975 to five in 1983. The ACLU's National Prison Project remains the largest of these, with eight attorneys and a budget of $1 million. Five others responded to the survey: Florida Institutional Legal Services, the Legal Action Center in New York, Massachusetts Correctional Legal Services, the Prison Law Clinic at Rutgers University Law School, and the Southern Prisoners Defense Committee.

The need for prisoners' rights centers is clear. The number of prisoners in the country is at an all-time high: over 500,000 in 1985, double the amount of ten years ago. Prison capacity has not kept up with the increase, and thirty-five states are currently under court orders to end overcrowding in their prisons, largely because of the efforts of these centers.[12]

Yet prison conditions are better than they were a decade ago, according to Alvin Bronstein, Executive Director of the National Prison Project. The Project is devoting most of its energies to monitoring the numerous court decrees calling for states to improve living conditions. Prisoners' rights lawyers are also working to outlaw the death penalty, eliminate employment barriers faced by ex-offenders, and ensure adequate care, particularly for prisoners with AIDS.[13]

Prison groups are funded primarily by foundation grants. Public contributions are not dependable, and government support is not an option for most, as the government continues to be an adversary in their cases. Attorneys' fees are being awarded more frequently in prison litigation and now constitute 25 percent of overall funding for this category. The Prison Project, for example, received $540,000 in 1983 for work in various cases.

Disability Law Centers

An important new category of groups addresses the needs of physically or mentally disabled persons. The Mental Health Law Project, which litigates and lobbies to advance the rights of the mentally impaired, was the only disability law firm identified in the 1975 survey. Today, there are fifteen such groups across the country, including Advocacy, Inc. (Austin, Texas), the Bay Area Center for Law and the Deaf (San Leandro, California), and the Community Health Law Project (East Orange, New Jersey).

The federal and state governments are the major funders of these centers, accounting for 73 percent of their combined budgets. Foundation funding, on the other hand, has been scarce, providing only 13 percent. Evan Kemp, Executive Director of the Disability Rights Center, expressed frustration with the philanthropic community. Foundations "do not have a separate category of giving for the disabled, and tend to fund special services" rather than advocacy or self-help projects.[14]

In addition to these centers, the federal government funds a network of "protection and advocacy" groups in every state. They provide individual services to those in mental health and retardation facilities and advocate on their behalf against abuse and neglect.

Disability rights centers in a short period of time have changed public policy on the disabled by bringing litigation that focuses on the widespread discrimination against them. During the 1970s, Congress passed the Rehabilitation Act and the Civil Rights of the Handicapped Act, which bar discrimination on the basis of handicap in any federally funded program or facility. In 1975, as a result of several court decisions declaring that handicapped children have a constitutional right to an education, Congress enacted the Education for All Handicapped Children Act, which guarantees those children a free, appropriate education in the least restrictive setting possible. For the past several years, disability rights advocates have brought litigation to clarify many of the Act's provisions.

Other Centers

A number of groups have recently formed to serve a variety of underrepresented individuals, including gays and lesbians, low income workers, and the elderly. The Lambda Legal Defense and Education Fund, founded in 1973 to represent homosexuals, has been joined by four other gay rights centers: the American Association for Personal Privacy, Gay/Lesbian Advocates and Defenders, the Lesbian Rights Project, and National Gay Rights Advocates. Although they have had difficulty in obtaining funding, these centers have raised enough money from individual contributors and membership dues to maintain active litigation programs. Recent work has focused on challenging workplace discrimination against people with AIDS.

Two legal centers serve low income or minority workers. The Employment Law Center, a project of the Legal Aid Society of San Francisco, helps disadvantaged people secure and retain employment. It recently represented a woman who returned to work after maternity leave to find that her job had not been held as promised; a man who lost his city job when it was discovered that he had once had cancer; and black employees who were paid less than white workers for the same work. The Industrial Cooperative Association in Somerville, Massachusetts develops worker-owned and worker-controlled businesses in low-income, minority, and blue collar communities.

The three groups defending the rights of the elderly include Legal Counsel for the Elderly, Legal Services for the Elderly, and the National Senior Citizens Law Center, a legal services backup center. They work primarily with federal agencies and Congress to improve health care, employment opportunities, welfare programs, and civil rights enforcement, particularly for the most vulnerable elderly: women, minorities, and the disabled.

Environmental Law Centers

As in 1975, the environmental law field is still dominated by three large national organizations: the Environmental Defense Fund (EDF), the Natural Resources Defense Council (NRDC), and the Sierra Club Legal Defense Fund (SCLDF). The National Wildlife Federation (NWF), the oldest environmental organization, also operates a substantial advocacy program. In 1983, 90 percent of all funding for environmental law went to these four centers.

Many of the newer centers operate at the state and local levels. The Legal Environmental Assistance Fund in Atlanta, Georgia, the Southern Environmental Law Center in Charlottesville, Virginia, the Conservation Law Foundation of New England in Boston, and Trustees for Alaska in Juneau, Alaska, all address local environmental concerns.

Environmental organizations rely less on foundation support than they did a decade ago. In a conscious attempt to diversify their funding bases, many centers launched aggressive membership drives and direct mail campaigns. In 1981, the National Audubon Society sent out a letter announcing that it was "entering a battle" with the federal government to prevent "the irrevocable destruction of much of America's natural heritage." The appeal raised almost $1 million in donations.[15] Other efforts have been similarly successful, particularly during the early eighties, when fundraising appeals targeted James Watt's prodevelopment activities during his tenure as Secretary of the Interior. Contributions from the public now account for more than half of the total funding for environmental groups, while the proportion supplied by foundation grants has dropped to 26 percent.

An active citizen base supports and augments the work of environmental law centers. This constituency has evolved over the years from consisting primarily of outdoor enthusiasts to those concerned with the protection of natural resources. Membership has surged since the 1970s: the National Audubon Society has more than doubled in size over this period, and the NRDC projected that by the end of 1987 it will have quadrupled its 1975 membership from 18,200 to 70,000.

Environmental organizations rely heavily on litigation to achieve their goals, although they also devote substantial time to monitoring federal and state administrative agencies to ensure that environmental statutes are being implemented properly. They have also sharply expanded their lobbying programs. NRDC and NWF, for instance, have successfully built coalitions with non-environmental groups to undertake legislative campaigns. The "green lobby," as it is called, has scored many congressional victories, including retention of strong clean air and water acts and extension of the Endangered Species Act. As the *National Law Journal* recently noted, "environmental advocacy has become a force to be reckoned with in every state and region."[16]

Consumer Law Centers

Three consumer law groups now dominate the scene: Ralph Nader's Public Citizen, Inc.; Consumers Union, the oldest consumer law center; and the Center for Science in the Public Interest. A number of the campus-based Public Interest Research Groups (PIRGs) also use lawsuits and lobbying campaigns to promote responsive government intervention in the marketplace.

In the late seventies, the federal government supplied nearly 70 percent of the financial support for these groups. In the wake of the budget cutbacks of the early eighties, public contributions, membership dues, and revenues from sales of publications replaced the government as the leading source of funds for consumer organizations. Sales alone accounted for 31 percent of overall income. These centers have also benefited from sophisticated direct mail marketing programs that have tapped new groups of givers.

Consumer law centers are working on a broad range of issues, including product liability and the tort system, the health effects of toxic wastes, worker health and safety, and tax reform. An innovative program instituted by Public Citizen in 1983 established a group buying cooperative. "Buyers Up" contracts with local oil suppliers to deliver heating oil to members for less than market prices.

Consumer law centers' strategies have changed to reflect the political climate. Consumers Union, for example, is appearing less in the courts and administrative agencies because of a drop in the number of new regulations being passed. Instead, they are turning to Congress to bring public pressure to bear on the positions adopted by the business community and regulatory agencies and working for the enactment of strong consumer and environmental legislation. As Mark Silbergeld, Executive Director of Consumers Union's Washington, D.C., office, comments, "Congress is the only place that doesn't have cement in its ears."[17] Consumers' groups are also experimenting with regulatory negotiation as an alternative to litigation to establish product standards and settle lawsuits that challenge regulations.

Consumer lawyers and activists have outlined an ambitious agenda for themselves for the next decade. Ralph Nader, for example, has often spoken about the need to develop new ways for citizens to control vast resources, ranging from the airwaves used by radio and television to public lands. He has been singularly active in urging consumers to look beyond the Reagan years to fashion a more humane and responsive society. "Regaining control of what is ours," Nader says, is a major step in that direction.[18]

Multi-issue Law Centers

The number of groups included under this rubric increased from thirteen in 1975 to twenty-one in 1983, primarily because a number of centers which existed in the early seventies only recently expanded their legal programs sufficiently to qualify as public interest law centers under the Alliance's definition. These organizations do not focus exclusively on a single issue, but rather represent citizens on a variety of matters that have important public policy implications.

Over the past five years many of these centers have, for various reasons, narrowed the scope of their agendas. First, foundations have a definite preference for providing specific project funding rather than general support, and many centers consequently have scaled down the number of projects they undertake. Second, as issues have become more complex, requiring a greater degree of specialization, the generalist public interest lawyers have become experts in particular fields. Finally, with many more centers now than a decade ago, these firms have found it necessary to focus their efforts on fewer issues to avoid duplicating the work of single-issue centers.

The Center for Law and Social Policy (CLASP), the prototype multi-issue firm, now works exclusively on poverty, civil rights, and family law. Over the past few years, a number of its programs have spun off to become independent entities: the National Women's Law Center and the Occupational Safety and Health Law Center began as CLASP projects. Its lawyers have been leading advocates for civil rights for the disabled and have fought to preserve the Legal Services Corporation. Like most other centers in this category, CLASP has also altered its fundraising focus. Until recently, almost all of its financial support came from foundations. It now raises significant amounts from individual donors and corporations.

The Los Angeles-based Center for Law in the Public Interest (CLIPI) also has altered its agenda as it faces a new era in public interest law. CLIPI lawyers now investigate cases of illegal campaign contributions, fraud in government contracting, and mishandling of the storage of toxic waste.

CLIPI's unusual success in generating large attorneys' fees awards offers a promising model of self-sufficiency for the future. Fifteen years ago, its chief source of support was the Ford Foundation. Since then, it has earned over $4 million in fees from litigation in federal courts, by far the largest amount received by any public interest law firm, and in 1983 these awards provided half of the Center's total budget. Business and Professional People for the Public Interest (BPI) in Chicago and the Public Interest Law Center of Philadelphia have also secured substantial awards of legal fees. All of these groups, however, have experienced difficulty in obtaining fees in state courts, generally because judges at this level have been more reluctant than their federal counterparts to award fees and because losing defendants have refused to pay the awards.

Trial Lawyers for Public Justice (TLPJ), the newest general public interest law firm, was formed in 1982 to develop and use plaintiffs' damages litigation as an instrument to achieve public interest goals. The firm takes cases involving corporate and government misconduct and seeks substantial monetary damages to recompense the victim and deter the defendant from engaging in injurious conduct. TLPJ derives almost all its income from fee awards and expects to be entirely self-sufficient within the next few years.

CONSERVATIVE LEGAL CENTERS

With the establishment of the Pacific Legal Foundation (PLF) in 1973, a new breed of law firms, laying claim to the title of public interest, was born. PLF's founders generally represent the interests of the business community against what they view as excessive government regulation of industry. They hold traditional public interest legal centers, and particularly environmental organizations, largely responsible for this overregulation and see themselves as a balance to the influence such groups exercise over public policy.

These "business oriented" law centers arrived on the scene at about the same time that "New Right" think tanks, institutes, and foundations were being founded. In the mid-1970s, the business community, joined by activist conservative organizations and foundations, felt the need to address the erosion of public support for the "free enterprise system." This group was particularly frustrated with environmental and consumer organizations and sought to reverse their courtroom successes by forming litigation centers to defend the views and interests of business.

A California businessman and longtime friend of President Reagan active in this movement expressed his feelings this way:

> I loathe environmentalists. . . . I say we should preserve the redwoods, sure, maybe 100 acres of them to show the kids. Those environmentalists who talk about preserving wilderness in Alaska—how many goddamned bloody people will end up going there in the next hundred years to suck their thumbs and write poetry? . . . This country needs the oil. If my country doesn't come ahead of my view, then I don't think much of my country.[19]

In 1975, the National Legal Center for the Public Interest (NLCPI) was formed to recreate the model of PLF in other parts of the country, and over the next two years seven additional centers were established: the Capital Legal Foundation (Washington, D.C.), the Gulf Coast and Great Plains Legal Foundation (Kansas City), the Mid-America Legal Foundation (Chicago), the Mid-Atlantic Legal Foundation (Philadelphia), the Mountain States Legal Foundation (Denver), the New England Legal Foundation (Boston), and the Southeastern Legal Foundation (Atlanta). Lawyers for these conservative public interest law firms have undertaken litigation challenging such programs as affirmative action and federal regulation of all types of industries.

Another category of business oriented firms, which includes the Washington Legal Foundation (WLF) and the Moral Majority Legal Defense Fund, advances a broad agenda encompassing a larger number of social issues. WLF, for example, has published pamphlets supporting capital punishment and prayer in school and opposing abortion and the Legal Services Corporation. Its lawyers lobbied hard for William Bradford Reynolds' unsuccessful bid for Associate Attorney General. They represented Senators Hatch and Helms in their efforts to seek deployment of the MX missile and assisted eight Congressmen in litigation requesting that the death penalty be applied in the Walker spy ring case. The Foundation has a $2 million budget and a staff of fifteen, and refers to itself as "the nation's largest pro-free enterprise public interest litigation and legal policy center."[20]

In 1979, the Alliance's survey included seven conservative groups, as well as NLCPI. In 1983, however, only four of the twelve to which the Alliance sent questionnaires responded (and of these, only two provided financial information). The contrast in response rates suggests a change in conservative centers' perception of their place within the public interest community. The high rate of response in 1979 showed that during the seventies, the groups sought legitimacy by identifying themselves with traditional advocacy organizations. Under President Reagan, conservative law centers enjoyed increased influence and, not surprisingly, felt less need to find a niche for themselves in a community of traditional public interest law firms.

Initially, some conservative public interest lawyers expressed concern about the movement's ability to attract enthusiastic graduates unless it developed a cohesive philosophy based on conservative ideology. Michael Horowitz, former chief legal counsel for the Office of Management and Budget, argued in a 1980 report to the Scaife Foundation that conservative firms must seek to become "players in the larger clash of philosophies, a battle that will be won not in the courtroom but in the minds of legislators, judges, the media, and—ultimately—the American people."[21]

A year later, three law students founded the Federalist Society, an organization of conservative lawyers and students. The Society has close ties to a number of conservative judges, including Justice Antonin Scalia, and administration officials, including Edwin Meese, and has become a favored job pool for judicial clerkships, congressional staff, and government positions. In 1986, it had seventy campus chapters and lawyers' divisions in Washington, D.C., New York, Los Angeles, and Chicago, for a total membership of 2,000.[22]

The Reagan Administration has also drawn upon business oriented firms to fill top policymaking posts: Attorney General Meese was one of the founders of the Pacific Legal Foundation; Wendy Borcherdt, appointed to the Office of Presidential Personnel, served on PLF's Board of Trustees; and former Secretary of the Interior James Watt once directed the Mountain States Legal Foundation.

Nowhere are the differences between conservative and traditional legal centers more apparent than in the courtroom. The former are closely identified with industry and corporate interests. They oppose government regulations limiting the use of natural resources by private developers. In *Utah Wilderness Committee v. Exxon*, for example, the Mountain States Legal Foundation filed an *amicus* brief supporting Exxon's right to mine wilderness areas. They also opposed air and water pollution control measures and have advocated more extensive use of controversial pesticides. In a case involving highway safety measures, the PLF and the Center for Auto Safety were on opposite sides of the debate: the Foundation opposed the installation of airbags in automobiles, while the Center supported it.

Another major difference is funding. The conservative groups continue to rely principally on corporations for support. For example, in

1981 PLF received over $2 million in tax-deductible contributions from such companies as Southern Pacific (a large land-holding and development corporation), Fluor Corporation, Title Insurance Corporation, and the foundations of Gulf Oil, Coors, Ford, and ARCO. In its first year, the Mountain States Legal Foundation received contributions of $500 or more from each of 175 corporations.[23]

Three conservative foundations—the John M. Olin and Sarah Scaife Foundations and the J. Howard Pew Freedom Trust—also make sizeable grants to these groups. In 1981–82, these foundations had combined assets of $461 million, and each averaged $8.6 million in grants and contributions. By way of contrast, nine of the largest foundations contributing to public interest law centers controlled a total of $10 million in assets and disbursed less than $1 million on the average during the same period.[24]

The internal governing bodies of the two types of firms also differ. The boards of traditional centers are generally composed of community leaders, local lawyers, and academics. The boards of business-oriented groups, on the other hand, are dominated by corporate executives. Of the twenty-eight members of the Southeastern Legal Foundation's 1985–86 Board of Trustees, at least nineteen were affiliated with businesses or corporations, including South Central Bell, Pilot Oil Corporation, and Mississippi Power & Light Company.[25] In 1984, sixteen of the twenty-one members of the Mid-Atlantic Legal Foundation's legal advisory board were corporate counsel for such companies as Rockwell International, Consolidated Natural Gas, and Bethlehem Steel Corporation.[26]

Finally, questions have arisen as to the tax-exempt status of conservative legal centers. They claim exemption, as do traditional advocacy organizations, under Section 501(c)(3) of the Internal Revenue Code. In seeking to classify public interest legal groups, the IRS has stated that, in order to be exempt, they may only provide representation on issues where "the individuals or groups involved cannot afford competent private counsel," and that they may not "accept cases in which private persons have a sufficient economic interest in the outcome of the litigation to justify the retention of private counsel."[27]

However, according to Tulane Law School Professor Oliver Houck, who conducted a two-year study of the structure and activities of conservative public interest groups, there is often a clear convergence between their litigation and the interests of their financial supporters and board members. In some instances, they actually represent large corporations which could clearly afford to retain private counsel.

Professor Houck substantiates his claims by citing numerous cases in which a business public interest firm's directors and supporters had a direct financial stake in the firm's litigation. For example, the Pacific Legal Foundation participated in *Dow Chemical Corporation v. Blum,* in which companies such as Dow, Chevron, and U. S. Steel contested an EPA ban on certain pesticides. Houck points out that "Chevron is a major contributor to PLF, and is represented by two major private law firms with partners on PLF's Board of Trustees." In *Southern Appalachian Multiple Use Council v. Bergland,* the Southeastern Legal Foundation filed suit on behalf of commercial lumber and mining interests to challenge a federal decision to withdraw a large area of forest land from multiple usage while it was being considered for classification as a protected wilderness area. The president of the West Lumber Company, which had a clear interest in maintaining the multiple-use classification, was a major contributor to the Foundation and sat on its original Board of Trustees.[28]

Although conservative public interest firms flourished under the Reagan Administration, the future appears to be less than secure for some. According to a *Legal Times* article, "a number of the regional foundations have experienced some money problems." For example, Dan Burt resigned as Executive Director of the Capital Legal Foundation in January 1987, amid signs that the group was all but defunct.[29] Several commentators say that the Mountain States Legal Foundation also has recently encountered funding difficulties. Lawyers familiar with these groups say that some retrenchment is occurring. However, due to the fact that these organizations refused to provide financial data, it is difficult to assess their current funding situation or make any predictions about their future.

THE PRIVATE PUBLIC INTEREST BAR

The private public interest law firm is another viable and widely used model for public interest practice. A large number of lawyers interested in representing community groups, environmentalists, and civil rights plaintiffs have carved out successful private practices over the years. A recent survey of Louisiana law firms, for example, found thirty-four private public interest law firms employing 297 attorneys.[30] States such as California and New York have hundreds of these firms handling a wide variety of public interest litigation.

Many practitioners identify with "movement lawyers" such as Arthur Kinoy, Ramsey Clark, and William Kunstler, who for years have been involved in seeking political and social change on behalf of labor unions and civil rights groups. Today, progressive lawyers are challenging U.S. policy in Central America, assisting illegal aliens facing deportation and suing manufacturers of toxic wastes. Others represent victims of employment discrimination, Social Security claimants, and indigent clients. Clearly, the areas addressed by progressive and public interest lawyers overlap, and the concept of a "movement" or "people's" lawyer seems far less coherent than it was during the 1960s and early 1970s.

Some of the more radical lawyers on the Left are critical of their colleagues in mainstream public interest groups. For example, the growing Critical Legal Studies movement fosters scholarly debate on this and other important issues. A basic tenet of the movement is that law is simply a tool used by the wealthy and powerful to protect their own interests. While they probably would not decry the efforts of public interest advocates in protecting indigent clients from the abuses of an inherently unfair system, Critical Legal Studies scholars would still view lawyers who seek reform through existing legislative and judicial channels as (perhaps unwittingly) perpetuating an unjust social order.

Most public interest lawyers say that while their work is worthwhile and personally fulfilling, it entails considerable economic sacrifice. Their incomes are far below those earned by colleagues with similar experience, and they have fewer resources upon which to draw for their day-to-day activities. Most say that they have found it necessary to develop a mix of work, taking on some cases which will bring in a steady income rather than relying solely on fee-generating litigation. Profitable clients who are on the "right" side of issues—labor unions, progressive foundations, environmental groups—generally have more work than their in-house legal staffs can handle, and can retain the services of private practitioners. These organizations provide a "floor" for meeting everyday expenses. However, there are not enough of these clients who can afford to pay fees "up front," so competition for clients is keen.

Litigation, although brought in the least expensive way, may require many hours of work, and fees can run very high if the issues are complex and the legal process protracted. This situation often creates an enormous financial burden for both the client, who may require considerable time to raise the money, and the private public interest firm, which is left with a serious cash flow problem in the meantime. Nevertheless, says Gail Harmon of Harmon and Weiss, "we're very tolerant in terms of payment, especially for groups that pay their lawyers through bake sales."[31]

Despite the numerous statutes providing for the award of attorneys' fees to victorious clients in public interest cases, most firms do not base their practice solely on the expectation of such awards. Those that do have in common a precarious financial base due to long delays in payment and the contingent nature of fees. "Depending on court awards is not a reliable way to earn a living," says Florence Roisman, of Roisman, Reno and Cavanaugh.[32]

Moreover, firms cannot afford to bring civil rights or other kinds of public interest cases if fee awards do not compensate them above normal noncontingent hourly rates. Jerome B. Falk, Jr., past president of the Bar Association of San Francisco and a partner in a large San Francisco corporate law firm, testified that because of the substantial risk and the delay in payment, "a rule of thumb which we follow is that the anticipated fee, if successful, should be at least twice the value of the projected time to be expended at our regular hourly rates."[33]

Another problem faced by private practitioners is litigating against a large corporate firm. One lawyer who refers to himself as an "aging activist" complains that

> you are easy meat for the big firms. They slowly eat you alive with NEXIS, the ten associates, paralegals, night-shift secretaries, and the whole SAC-command infrastructure. They could drown you with paper every week. When they file a motion, say to dismiss your case, it is fiendishly timed to ruin your weekend—two feet of reading, dumped off at your office 5 p.m. Thursday, set for hearing 9 a.m. Monday.[34]

While some private lawyers wonder whether they should change careers, or transform their Title VII practices into medical malpractice firms, or go to work for nonprofit organizations, they do enjoy some advantages. Free from the constraints imposed on nonprofits by the IRS and by foundations, they have considerably more flexibility in their choice of litigation. Finally, because private public interest lawyers become known in a community for taking certain kinds of cases, "nobody ever comes in from the other side" to retain their services.[35] Unlike their counterparts in corporate firms, they do not have to take on work which may conflict with their principles.

THE PRIVATE BAR

A key recommendation in *Balancing the Scales of Justice*, a report by the Council for Public Interest on the development and financing of public interest law, called for increased involvement by the private bar in handling *pro bono* cases and in subsidizing legal services for the poor. In fact, the year that *Balancing* was published (1975) saw thousands of private attorneys devoting many hours to representing indigent and other public interest clients. The American Bar Association (ABA) sponsored committees to investigate ways to encourage its members to become involved in public interest work and to address problems of financing the legal representation of underrepresented individuals. For instance, the ABA Special Committee on Public Interest Law pressed for the adoption of attorneys' fees statutes and the appropriation of federal funds to enable citizen groups to participate in agency rulemaking procedures. It was also a time when many bright, enthusiastic law graduates chose public interest law, believing that private practice in a traditional law firm would not be fulfilling. Because of the substantial number of lawyers available to represent the disadvantaged, *Balancing* expressed the hope that by establishing such work within private law firms, public interest law itself would be institutionalized.

However, in the decade that followed, firms began to cut back their *pro bono* work. Because of the recession and inflation of the late seventies, many law firms experienced soaring overheads and increased competition from other firms. Consequently, they began to look more closely at their billable hours. As one lawyer describes it,

> Even my firm, which for thirty years has been known for its *pro bono* work, began to rein in our young lawyers—not by limiting their non-billable time, but by increasing the expectation for billable time. Thus, in most cases, the individual lawyer was left to decide whether to stay on track for partnership by putting in the expected billable time, whether to give to indigents, or whether to devote time to something that, for lawyers, often takes a backseat—his or her own family. We found that the choice was not hard for some of these young lawyers. The public spirited youngsters coming just out of school in the 1960's and 1970's has been replaced by a more conservative group of young lawyers, more attuned to their own economic survival than in the past.[36]

Other factors are also responsible for firms' declining concern with public interest law. First, firms are more selective in the types of cases they take, accepting only those cases or parties which do not present a conflict of interest with other clients. However, some public interest lawyers charge that firms interpret the term "conflict of interest" too broadly, and weed out clients or issues which might simply offend the paying clientele. Second, firms prefer work that can be disposed of quickly, and thus refrain from taking public interest cases, which often involve extensive factfinding and litigation. Finally, many of the legal problems of the poor and other disadvantaged groups involve complex issues and require specialized knowledge and skills. Inevitably, law firms lacking these skills shy away from such cases.

A more conservative political climate and a greater adherence to the "bottom line" notwithstanding, some firms and bars continue to carry a heavy *pro bono* practice, primarily in the form of legal assistance to the poor. For example, after cutbacks in funding for the Legal Services Corporation in 1982, many lawyers responded to calls for the private bar to handle more cases for indigent clients, and bar associations across the country developed programs to work with *pro bono* providers. Considerably less is being done by private firms with regard to policy-oriented public interest issues, but there are a handful of bar-sponsored programs and firms willing to take on this sort of work. The Los Angeles Bar sponsors a public interest law firm called Public Counsel, which concentrates on First Amendment, environmental law, and minority employment cases. Other city bars have formed panels of volunteer attorneys that focus on domestic relations, bankruptcy, the elderly, and the homeless. In New York City, lawyers both fund and are referred *pro bono* work by New York Lawyers for the Public Interest.

Other developments suggest a renewed enthusiasm for public interest law on the part of the organized bar. Lawyers across the country are contributing in large numbers to client trust funds, designed to provide financial support to legal services and public interest organizations. Others are making themselves more available to take *pro bono* cases. As one lawyer commented, "I'm an attorney. I took an oath in which this obligation is implied, if not stated."[37]

Notes

1. Giles R. Scofield, Trustee, New York University Public Interest Law Foundation, "Public Interest Law, Energy and the Economy" (Letters to the Editor), *Wall Street Journal* (December 31, 1979), p. 7.

2. Robert L. Gnaizda, Senior Attorney, Public Advocates, Inc., as quoted in Oliver A. Houck, "With Charity for All," 93 *The Yale Law Journal* 8 (July 1984), p. 1544.

3. Although referred to separately in the previous chapter, these two program types are grouped together here because of their common interests and clients.

4. "Civil Rights, Social Justice and Black America." A Ford Foundation Working Paper (New York: The Ford Foundation, 1984), p. 50.

5. Alliance for Justice interview with Burton Fretz, Executive Director, National Senior Citizens Law Center, July 20, 1984.

6. Alliance interview with Bucky Askew, Staff Attorney, National Legal Aid and Defenders Association, February 13, 1987.

7. Anita Arriola and Sidney Wolinsky, "Public Interest Practice in Practice: The Law and Reality," 34 *Hastings Law Journal* (May–July, 1983), p. 1207.

8. Linda E. Demkovich, "FRAC: A Lean, Mean Hunger Machine Fueled by Research, Action and Controversy," 16 *National Journal* 1 (January 1, 1984), p. 169.

9. Two of the fifteen groups did not provide information on the number of attorneys employed.

10. *Financial Support of Women's Programs in the 1970s.* A Report to the Ford Foundation (New York: The Ford Foundation, 1979), pp. 7, 15.

11. *Ibid.*, pp. 18, 12.

12. Saundra Saperstein, "District Not Alone In Prison Crisis," *Washington Post*, July 20, 1986, p. A1.

13. Alliance for Justice interview with Alvin Bronstein, Executive Director of the National Prison Project, December 22, 1983.

14. Alliance for Justice interview with Evan Kemp, Executive Director of the Disability Rights Center, September 14, 1984.

15. William Symonds, "The Grip of the Green Giant," *Fortune Magazine*, vol. 106 (October 4, 1982), p. 138.

16. Ezra Tom Clark, Jr., "The Key to a Firm's Financial Success," *National Law Journal* (June 18, 1984), pp. 25, 33.

17. Alliance for Justice interview with Mark Silbergeld, Executive Director, Washington D.C. office of Consumers Union, January 6, 1987.

18. Address by Ralph Nader, "Looking Ahead: The Future of Public Interest Law," to the Alliance for Justice's conference, Preserving Access to Justice, June 11, 1985.

19. Justin Dart, quoted in Williams, "Farewell to a Forest," *Boston Magazine*, p. 133.

20. Daniel J. Popeo, "General Counsel's Message," Washington Legal Foundation *Annual Report 1985*, p. 1.

21. Michael J. Horowitz as quoted in Houck, "With Charity," p. 1513.

22. "Judge Scalia's Cheerleaders," *New York Times*, July 23, 1986, p. 10.

23. Houck, "With Charity," pp. 1462, 1478.

24. David M. Gordon, "Up From the Ashes—III: Where's the Money Coming From?," *The Nation*, vol. 240, no. 7 (February 23, 1985), p. 206.

25. Board of Trustees as listed in the Southeastern Legal Foundation *Annual Report, 1985–1986.*

26. Houck, "With Charity," p. 1495.

27. Rev. Ruling 75–74, 1975, as quoted in Houck, "With Charity," p. 1453.

28. Houck, "With Charity," pp. 1469, 1500.

29. Eric Effron, "Legal Group Dwindling As Burt Surrenders Reins," *Legal Times*, vol. IX, no. 33 (January 26, 1987), pp. 1, 5.

30. Tulane Law School Office of Career Services, *Public Interest Career Guide, 1986–87*, pp. 27–33.

31. Gail Harmon of Harmon and Weiss, as quoted in Steve Nelson, "Private Public Interest Firms Establish Bases," *Legal Times*, vol. IV, no. 45 (April 19, 1982), p. 32.

32. Alliance for Justice interview with Florence Roisman of Roisman, Reno and Cavanaugh, April 3, 1987.

33. Jerome B. Falk, "Declaration in Support of Plaintiffs' Application for Interim Award of Attorneys' Fees," Plaintiffs' Exhibit 5 at 4:10–5:1, *Kraszewski v. State Farm General Insurance Co.*, Docket No. C79–1261 TEH (N.D. Cal. Dec. 15, 1985).

34. Thomas Geoghegan, "Warren Court Children," *The New Republic*, issue 3,722 (May 19, 1986), p. 17.

35. Bruce Terris of Terris and Sunderland, as quoted in Nelson, "Private Public Interest Firms," p. 330.

36. Patricia D. Phillips, "Financing the Right to Counsel: A View from the Private Bar," *Right to Counsel*, vol. 19 (December 1985), p. 379.

37. Erica Wood and Susan Love, "Corporate Lawyers Go *Pro Bono*," 70 *American Bar Association Journal* (August 1984), p. 77.

5

Litigation and Other Social Change Strategies

Although litigation remains a carefully used instrument, there is still no other strategy that can shake the foundation of an institution.[1]

Litigation remains the one arena in which we can equal and sometimes even succeed our opponents.[2]

THE BROAD DIVERSITY OF STRATEGIES

Over the past several years, public interest lawyers have diversified their strategies to bring about social change. At the same time, they have broadened their focus to include more actions at the state and local levels. Today, in addition to pursuing litigation and administrative advocacy, public interest law firms typically engage in such varied activities as legislative advocacy (often carried out through coalition efforts); monitoring policy formation and implementation by regulatory agencies; public education about the issues through the organization's own publications and the media; and advising and counseling individuals.

Such was not always the case. During the 1960s and early 1970s, public interest law organizations relied on forums such as the courts and administrative agencies to protect the rights of unrepresented persons and groups and to enforce public health and civil rights statutes. Encouraged by the judicial victories achieved by the American Civil Liberties Union (ACLU) and the NAACP Legal Defense and Education Fund (NAACP/LDF) in removing barriers to equal treatment, a wide variety of new public interest law organizations, including the Natural Resources Defense Council, the Women's Legal Defense Fund, the Mental Health Law Project, the Center for Law and Social Policy (CLASP), and the Center for Law in the Public Interest (CLIPI), turned to the courts to represent new interests and emerging constituencies.

Indeed, some groups, such as the Environmental Defense Fund, were virtually created in the courtroom.

In the early years, the lack of resources meant that public interest lawyers' first priority was filing lawsuits. Organizations had neither the staff nor the financial backing to fashion comprehensive solutions to problems. Dozens of legal actions were filed to enforce the National Environmental Policy Act and the substantive provisions of other protective environmental legislation, such as clean air and water laws. Other litigation aimed at improving standards of medical care for the poor, protecting consumers, desegregating housing, and enforcing fair employment practices for women and minorities. Much of this litigation was highly visible, often resulting in dramatic changes at the community level. Groups challenged major government or corporate actions: the proposed construction of highways, pipelines, or dams; import quotas on basic commodities such as steel and oil; and proposed mergers of large corporations or banks.

Once the movement got underway, public interest lawyers frequently found it easier to accomplish their objectives by presenting their views in administrative forums rather than by bringing lawsuits. Much effort was aimed at prodding the federal government to exercise its regulatory powers more vigorously. The Center for National Policy Review, for example, successfully pushed to get detailed affirmative action regulations adopted by federal agencies for their internal workings and for programs that the government helped to fund. Public interest lawyers petitioned such agencies as the Securities and Exchange Commission, the Coast Guard, the Civil Aeronautics Board, and the Environmental Protection Agency to strengthen their regulations in ways designed to benefit the public. Many agency officials regularly sought the expertise of public interest lawyers for assistance in evaluating existing regulations, in assessing priorities for action, and in shaping the substance of new regulatory programs.

The staffing patterns of public interest law firms reflected this almost exclusive focus on the courts and administrative agencies. Firms employed primarily lawyers and secretaries, with only minor participation by the types of professionals typically working at other nonprofit groups. As Charles Halpern, founder of CLASP, notes:

> What we had in mind was setting up an institution that would provide services to unrepresented groups which were similar in kind to the services provided by an ordinary law firm. Our emphasis was on courts and administrative agencies. We thought of ourselves as legal advocates, not as people who were organized as a community organization, not as

people who were part of the political process except in a very peripheral way.

We were doing what Covington and Burling was doing for corporate clients, except we were doing it for citizens' organizations: for poor people, for civil rights groups, for neighborhood development corporations, for consumer and environmental groups. We did not align ourselves with any particular group, but saw ourselves as lawyers offering a particular service, generally without cost, to groups who couldn't afford to buy legal services.[3]

Recognizing that the political environment of the late 1970s required new strategies, the public interest community quickly mobilized and reconsidered their former reliance on litigation and agency-oriented activities. In part, public interest lawyers were the victims of their own successes. Their legal victories led to counterattacks from affected interests such as corporations, trade associations, philosophical conservatives, antifeminists, and right-wing religious groups like the Moral Majority. The targets of public interest litigation fought back harder, escalating legal costs in the process and requiring the adoption of new strategies.

Relations between public interest lawyers and federal regulatory agencies cooled under the Reagan Administration. The Administration's deregulation and domestic retrenchment policies threatened many of the gains of the 1960s and 1970s, making it necessary for public interest lawyers to work more closely with community groups to elicit their support in lobbying Congress and to appeal more directly to public opinion. The relaxation of lobbying rules allowed these organizations to seek redress through the legislative process as well.

Today, while litigation and participation in government proceedings still constitute much of their workload, public interest groups have diversified their tactics and activities. To accomplish these new tasks, they have recruited lobbyists, community organizers, researchers, and budget analysts to their staffs, and lawyers themselves have expanded their range of knowledge and skills to function more effectively in the changed political environment.

Legislative Advocacy

During the past two decades, environmental, civil rights, consumer, children's, and senior citizens' organizations have lobbied Congress to enact or strengthen public health and civil rights laws. Working in coalitions with churches, labor unions, and community organizations around the country, public interest lawyers have struggled to achieve the political leverage necessary to push through new legislative programs benefiting the public.

The hostility of the Reagan Administration to many of the goals of the public interest community, however, made it even more important for the public interest law movement to learn how to lobby potentially sympathetic forces in Congress. As Michael Pertschuk, former Commissioner of the Federal Trade Commission and a lobbyist himself, comments, "The Reagan assault hastened the professionalization of public interest lobbying." Although "still modest in numbers, the corps of public interest lobbyists" has achieved in recent years "a new level of expertise and sophistication."[4]

Over the years, lobbying has become a widely accepted form of advocacy work. As Mr. Pertschuk notes, the classic stereotype of the Washington lobbyist who engages in influence peddling and runs up huge entertainment bills while supposedly "working" social contacts has been joined by a new, less monied, but more serious breed. Once accustomed to playing a behind-the-scenes role, preparing legal memoranda for use by citizen lobbies, public interest organizations are themselves taking up legislative advocacy.

Veteran public interest lawyers are now widely recognized for their expertise in environmental, civil rights, and consumer law. They are regularly consulted by members of Congress and congressional staff for information and advice. Over the years such interaction has put some of the "tools of the trade" of the lobbyist—an extensive set of personal contacts on the Hill, knowledge of who the decisionmakers are, and an understanding of the policy-making process—in the hands of public interest lawyers.

Working in Coalitions

For the public interest community, lobbying is largely an aspect of coalition work. What public interest lobbyists lack in financial resources they often more than make up for through informed networks of organizations and concerned citizens. Over the past several years, public interest groups have formed an unprecedented number of coalitions, both formal and *ad hoc*. Some formal coalitions, such as the Leadership Conference on Civil Rights, are supported by dues-paying member organizations to coordinate lobbying strategies on civil rights issues. More typically, *ad hoc* alliances form around specific issues and then disappear once the issue is resolved. Groups have found that a broad coalition gives their cause greater credibility in Congress. Working with other groups also enables public interest organizations, which are restricted in the amount of lobbying they may undertake, to expand their scope of influence in the critical legislative arena.

Public interest centers often serve as the legal arm and adviser to coalitions. The National Senior Citizens Law Center (NSCLC), for example, works with the American Association of Retired Persons, the National Council on the Aging, the National Council of Senior Citizens, and other organizations in the Leadership Council of Aging Organizations, a coalition that has emerged as a powerful voice for the elderly. According to NSCLC Executive Director Burton Fretz, his organization advises the Leadership Council on the legal implications of its actions and provides analyses of existing laws, proposed legislation, and administrative agency rulemakings.[5] Similarly, the Institute for Public Representation served as coordinator and chief legal adviser to the fifty-five member Voting Access Coalition that lobbied in support of the Voting Accessibility for the Elderly and Handicapped Act. Passed in 1984, the Act requires all polling places and a reasonable number of voter registration facilities to be accessible to elderly and disabled voters.

Coalition work aimed at influencing Congress, federal agencies, and state legislatures will undoubtedly remain an integral component of public interest activity. Only coalition activity can overcome the political, legal, and practical constraints on any one group to carry out a legislative campaign.

Unlikely Allies

Unusual alliances may develop in the course of such legislative advocacy. For example, in 1981, the steel industry and environmental groups jointly asked a Senate committee to act quickly on legislation to give businesses three additional years to meet clean air standards. The proposal allowed companies to spend antipollution monies on modernizing plants, rather than on installing pollution control devices on outmoded equipment.

In another unusual alliance, this time in the regulatory arena, the Environmental Defense Fund (EDF) joined several large oil companies in 1982 in opposing efforts by the Environmental Protection Agency (EPA) and small oil refiners to raise the acceptable level of lead in gasoline. Together, EDF and the oil companies presented scientific studies showing that airborne lead can cause brain damage in children and persuaded EPA to forgo changes in the existing regulations.

Pursuing joint legislative strategies can be mutually advantageous to the corporate and the public interest communities. By working with public interest lobbyists, businesses gain a measure of credibility and additional congressional contacts. On the other hand, businesses provide additional financial resources, technical assistance, and access to certain members of Congress. Nonetheless, public interest groups enter into coalitions with businesses and trade associations cautiously. Aware of the differences in advocacy styles and approaches, and fearful of being co-opted or forced into unacceptable compromises, they weigh the pros and cons carefully before taking on such joint efforts.

Lobbying and Litigation

Legislative advocacy and litigation often go hand in hand. Cases won in the courts may be in danger of being overturned by laws later enacted by Congress. For example, in 1970 the Center for Law and Social Policy successfully challenged in the courts the construction of the Alaska gas pipeline. After this victory, Congress passed a bill permitting construction to continue.

On the other hand, cases lost in the courts may spur remedial congressional action. In 1985 the National Wildlife Federation unsuccessfully challenged in court the Department of Interior's sale of coal leases in Montana and Wyoming at less-than-market rates. The Federation argued that this practice of underselling had resulted in the loss to the federal treasury of millions of dollars and was threatening precious natural resources with destruction. By bringing these practices to light, the court action, although unsuccessful, sparked a furor in the press and focused public attention and Congressional scrutiny on the government's coal leasing program. Members of Congress consulted with the Federation in designing legislative action to stop the sales. A commission was established to evaluate the government's coal leasing program and a moratorium on future sales was passed. "The relationship between the litigation and Hill action was like synergy," recalls Federation counsel Norman Dean, "and the media attention to the litigation and congressional committee reports was important to the outcome on the Hill."[6]

Consumer advocate Ralph Nader believes that the legislature is as crucial an arena for the practice of public interest law as the courts: "There is just no way that a unilateral advance of public interest advocacy can occur just in the courts—you have to deal with the adversary on all the fronts on which the adversary deals with you." This is the reason, explained Nader, that when he organized the Public Citizen Litigation Group, he also set up Congress Watch and other legislation-oriented efforts. Through such a multiplicity of efforts, public interest groups "try to provide a broad front of advance, because you can't do it [effectively defend the public interest] with just one narrow probe utilizing one branch of government. Sooner or later, the counterattack will come through another branch of government."[7]

Publishing and Publicity

Because the process of affecting public policy depends so much on information, public interest centers engage in a variety of activities designed to present facts and research to the public. Many groups publish newsletters on a regular basis and periodically release specialized studies, investigative reports, or how-to handbooks for concerned citizens. These publications may detail the harms or benefits to the public of various government policies, present empirical data relevant to an issue or discuss its historical background.

Groups have become much more sophisticated about the potential of media to convey their messages. The successful employment of television and radio by the religious right, as well as by corporations, spurred public interest groups to expand their own use of these tools. The substantial growth in membership and outreach activities of public interest groups has also made it necessary for them to take advantage of recent advances in telecommunications. Through publicity and publications, public interest law groups have offered their expertise and point of view to concerned citizens and those affected by government policies.

Publication Activities

The publications of legal groups provide advocates with information that is not easily obtainable elsewhere and present it in a format that lay persons can understand and use. For example, *The Citizen Handbook on Groundwater Protection*, published by the Natural Resources Defense Council (NRDC), gives citizens and public officials background material on current issues so that they may act as informed advocates for better groundwater protection policies. Another NRDC publication, *Children's Art Hazards*, alerts teachers and parents to the health hazards posed by commonly available art materials. The Mental Health Law Project, the Food Research and Action Center, and other legal services support centers compiled a handbook on federal and state entitlement programs for use by operators of charitable soup kitchens, emergency shelter providers, and other advocates for homeless people.

A broad range of newsletters, from *Youth Law News* of the National Center for Youth Law to *Nutrition Action Health Letter* of the Center for Science in the Public Interest, keeps members and friends abreast of an organization's current activities, upcoming government actions, and emerging issues in the field. Sometimes these newsletters become important tools in mobilization efforts. For example, in a 1982 issue of its newsletter, *Update*, the Mental Health Law Project described a newly adopted Social Security Administration policy which terminated the benefits of many mentally ill people by classifying them as capable of supporting themselves through paid employment. The story drew a tremendous response from newsletter readers, who told the Project about cases of benefits being terminated under this dubious rationale. Some of these newsletter story contacts eventually became plaintiffs in a successful challenge brought by the Project to what it termed a "clandestine policy" to change eligibility criteria. A federal appeals court in New York ordered the federal government to restore benefits that had been denied to 50,000 mentally ill people in the state, and a few months later Congress passed the Disability Benefits Reform Act of 1984, which forbade such cutoffs.[8]

Media Efforts

Public interest lawyers also use the mass media to educate clients, constituents, and the public at large about current issues. "Publicity is an important means to many of the ends that public interest lawyers seek on behalf of their client groups," notes Carlyle Hall, Jr., Executive Director of the Center for Law in the Public Interest. It "can have a profound effect on the outcome and significance of a legal action."[9]

Of course, most public interest legal groups lack the financial resources necessary to fund an advertising media blitz of the sort seen in, for example, a political campaign. However, they have become quite adept at accessing the "free media" of broadcast and print journalism. Many journalists recognize the expertise of public interest lawyers and call on them for comment on various issues or invite them to appear on public affairs programs. Some organizations have also successfully used radio and television public service announcements. The Women's Legal Defense Fund, for example, launched an extensive media campaign in 1982. "It Pays to Be a Man," aired in ten cities across the country, aimed to increase public understanding and acceptance of the concept of equal pay for work of comparable worth.

Advice and Counseling

Increasing numbers of minorities, women, disabled persons, and other disadvantaged groups who cannot afford a private lawyer are turning to public interest law centers for counseling. With fewer government resources and programs to provide assistance, public interest lawyers are in some instances the only sources of information about available legal resources or about the options—legal and nonlegal— available to injured individuals.

The Women's Legal Defense Fund, for example, receives more than 6,000 calls a year for legal assistance.[10] Equal Rights Advocates in San Francisco has instituted an advice and counseling program to respond to the hundreds of calls each year from women who believe they have been victims of sexual discrimination and need information and guidance.

Some organizations have installed hotlines to handle the volume of public inquiries. The Center for Public Representation in Madison, Wisconsin, developed the Medigap hotline, which counsels senior citizens on the purchase of supplemental health insurance. The program proved so popular that the Board on Aging and Long Term Care was founded to continue it. The Natural Resources Defense Council maintains a toll-free Toxics Hotline, which provides information about hazardous substances to anyone concerned about possible exposure or seeking accurate information on toxic substances.

Action at the Local Level

Public interest law continues to maintain a major presence in the capital, working to influence national policy in the federal courts, agencies, and Congress, but it is no longer solely a Washington phenomenon. There are also clusters of centers across the country and more than two dozen public interest firms which now maintain litigation and advocacy work almost entirely at the state or local level.

In San Francisco, for example, such locally focused public interest law organizations as Equal Rights Advocates, Public Advocates, Inc., and the Employment Law Center of the Legal Aid Society of San Francisco work on a broad range of concerns: the treatment of migrant workers; consumer protection; conditions in public institutions; and the welfare of children, women, minorities, and the elderly. In Philadelphia, organizations such as the Juvenile Law Center, the Women's Law Project, and the Education Law Center work extensively in their own special subject areas and also "meet together on a regular basis" because "so much of the casework overlaps," according to Robert Schwartz, Executive Director of the sixteen-year-old Juvenile Law Center. These organizations are becoming an "institutionalized" part of the local legal scene, even as "other private lawyers come and go," says Mr. Schwartz. The Center spends most of its time in collaborative efforts with the city and state child welfare and juvenile justice systems, although it does undertake litigation, particularly at the state level.[11]

Often the litigation that such local groups bring has important regional or even national impact. In the environmental area, for example, Business and Professional People for the Public Interest, a public interest law firm in Chicago, played a key role in formulating environmental safeguards and financial protections for the State of Illinois as part of a revised Midwest Compact, an interstate agreement designating a regional disposal site for low-level radioactive wastes.

Other cases brought by local public interest lawyers have had national implications. The Center for Law in the Public Interest, based in Los Angeles, filed a suit hailed by Neil Goldschmidt, former U.S. Secretary of Transportation, as a "precedent for the rest of the United States, against the seventeen-mile, $1.2 billion Century Freeway."[12] The litigation was settled when the Department of Transportation agreed to redesign the freeway, providing rapid transit and other environmental design features, and further agreed to use federal gas tax funds to construct thousands of low-income housing units to replace affordable housing lost due to the freeway's construction.

The movement over the past few years to transfer responsibility for the poor and disadvantaged from the federal to the state governments has caused many national public interest organizations to focus more sharply on what the states are doing and to hold state programs to the same standards as federal ones. With decisions about the allocation of public funds also shifting from Washington to the states, national centers are working directly with local community groups. These organizations are mobilizing citizens to monitor the enforcement of federal policies at the state level and to influence the disbursement of block grant funds in order to protect vital human services.

To further their work at the state level, some organizations, including the Children's Defense Fund, the Environmental Defense Fund, and the National Wildlife Federation, have opened regional branches in recent years. Other organizations are involved in projects in the cities where they are headquartered. For instance, the Natural Resources Defense Council's Urban Environment Project, which focuses on New York City, lobbied for the multi-billion dollar transit rebuilding program currently underway.

Although the clients and issues may be local, the results of public interest legal actions often can be replicated in other communities. In 1985, for example, when a county planning commission in Kentucky was considering changes in zoning laws that would have made it more difficult to operate group homes for mentally and physically handicapped people in certain neighborhoods, the Mental Health Law Project testified on behalf of a coalition of group home operators. The Project's testimony helped persuade the planning commission to defer any firm action on the proposed changes. The Project described this success story in *Update*, its newsletter, and received requests for their testimony and supporting studies from hundreds of group home operators and other citizens interested in the issue.[13]

"We will be seeing more action on the state and local level," believes Peter Forsythe, Vice President of the Edna McConnell Clark Foundation, which funds many public interest law projects. "The model of national programs moving out to the local areas is the model of the future."[14] Yet, funding problems have certainly slowed the growth of this localizing process, and have even caused setbacks. Nancy Amidei, formerly of the Food Research and Action Center (FRAC), comments that the network of legal groups capable of carrying on nutrition advocacy at the state level "has dissipated." Community action programs and legal services agencies have been defunded, leaving national organizations such as FRAC with many more responsibilities to carry out at all levels of government.[15]

Monitoring and Influencing
Actions of Federal Agencies

Public interest centers have broadened their scope of advocacy beyond the courts and agencies. However, monitoring the activities of the federal administrative agencies remains a significant part of the work of such groups. It involves both keeping an eye on the agencies where policy decisions are made and staying in close communication with the lawyers and citizen groups concerned about agency policies. At the national level, public interest lawyers have developed an informal network of those interested in and affected by the actions of certain agencies. Lawyers obtain and review early drafts of regulatory changes, passing them along for comment. This early warning system enables concerned organizations to mobilize quickly against potentially adverse agency actions.

Although public interest groups continue to rely to some extent on internal agency contacts and informal participation in agency decisionmaking, they have enjoyed far less access to agency processes and officials during the Reagan Administration than under previous administrations. Consequently, bringing public pressure to bear on key policy decisions has become an even more crucial tactic in recent years. More than ever, public interest lawyers today must play the watchdog and raise public alarms when adverse actions are pending or important issues are being neglected. Given the wide-ranging deregulation efforts of the Reagan Administration and the vast number of rule changes it has proposed and implemented, there has been a great need to help citizen groups understand the implications of agency proposals. However, the role played by public interest lawyers in the regulation process extends beyond just that of pushing an unwilling government. One environmental lawyer, Richard Mallory, noted that public interest groups can help to shift the balance inside an agency by providing a context in which people inside government who are sympathetic with the goals of a public interest group can promote their work. It is easier for a general counsel of an agency to announce a pro-environmental position if outside groups are actively supporting it.[16]

In recent years, agency enforcement of environmental statutes has become particularly lax. "The enforcement of environmental laws by the executive branch has all too frequently been weak and grudging," believes Frederic P. Sutherland, Executive Director of the Sierra Club Legal Defense Fund. "The agencies and officials charged with administering the laws have delayed, missed deadlines, attempted to convert mandatory standards to discretionary ones, created loopholes, watered down strict statutes through the use of the regulatory process, or simply refused to use their enforcement powers when faced with blatant violations of law."[17] Under such circumstances, the watchdog role of public interest lawyers becomes crucial.

One creative new effort to monitor and report on the evolution of national civil rights policies in the Reagan Administration was the formation of the Citizens' Commission on Civil Rights in 1982. Its purpose, according to Arthur Flemming, former Secretary of Health, Education, and Welfare and current Commission chairman, was to complement the oversight activities of the U.S. Commission on Civil Rights.[18] A series of reports by the Citizens' Commission focused public attention on attempts by the U.S. Commission on Civil Rights to narrow affirmative action regulations.

THE CRUCIAL ROLE OF LITIGATION

The public interest law movement clearly makes use of many strategies in fighting for social change. Advocates may canvass neighborhoods, talk to the press, arouse public opinion, lobby legislators, and prod regulatory agencies. They may forgo the adversarial relationships of the courtroom in favor of mediating a dispute. Nonetheless, litigation remains the crucial weapon in their arsenal. The ability to sue is the great equalizer among parties to a public interest law case. Even if no lawsuit is brought, it is often the record of past litigation successes that puts "teeth" into these other strategies.

Thus, although public interest firms do much more than take cases to court, and although their lawyers may choose from a variety of other strategies, litigation still remains the *sine qua non* of public interest law. After all, many kinds of professionals in different types of organizations can effectively educate, advocate, and lobby for a good cause, but it takes lawyers to harness the power of the judiciary in the struggle for social change. In many situations, litigation is the only hope of achieving success.

What Litigation Can Accomplish

Public interest litigation can spur recalcitrant regulatory agencies, public institutions, or businesses into action. It can enforce existing laws and regulations, even when those responsible for their implementation would rather ignore them. By raising constitutional issues, litigation can extend rights to new population groups and establish constitutional norms. Litigation can restructure public institutions by obtaining judicial decrees that demand protection or better care for prisoners, mental patients, and other institutionalized populations. In a complex society, where many interests compete, the courtroom provides a forum in which disputes may be compromised or settled fairly. Litigation empowers disadvantaged groups. Civil rights authority William L. Taylor writes that *Brown v. Board of Education*

> rekindled the hopes of black people and gave new energy to the programs of established organizations, notably the NAACP. When *Brown* was not enforced because our national leaders lacked the political will, hope and anger combined to fuel the direct action protest movement led by Dr. King. And that movement was the catalyst for the breakthroughs of the 1960s—the civil rights laws that not only declared an official end to the caste system that had prevailed for two centuries but provided tools to enable people to remove barriers of discrimination from their own lives. In the years since, the fruits of empowerment can be seen everywhere. They are perhaps most visible on the political scene, in the election of black candidates to office, which can be traced directly to the Voting Rights Act and important court decisions, in the confidence that these laws and decisions inspired in black people and in the political organization and hard work that followed. The fruits of *Brown* can also be seen in economic empowerment, in educational empowerment and in the roles that large numbers of black people play in hundreds of professional associations, community organizations and other centers of influence— roles that were almost unheard of thirty years ago.
>
> In sum, the implicit message of the *Brown* decision was that by their own efforts even the people most discriminated against in this society could make the system work for them. If it is sadly true that the message still rings hollow in 1985 for millions of black people who are worse off in this country, for many, many others, *Brown* was the event that ultimately enabled them to gain control over their own lives.[19]

Litigation provides a community with a way to say "no" to a proposed project—a hazardous nuclear power plant, or a freeway—that it does not like. A court case can strengthen a community by bringing concerned parties together and can greatly aid in consolidating organizational efforts. Litigation also plays a very important educational function, raising consciousness through discussion of the issues, changing public opinion, and making possible progress toward a more just society.

Choosing Cases and Tactics

Some of the most important accomplishments of public interest law have resulted from sustained litigation campaigns; the series of anti-segregation law suits brought by the NAACP Legal Defense and Education Fund that climaxed in the *Brown* decision is the classic example. Beginning with lawsuits to admit black students to all-white state law schools in 1939, this campaign built a series of precedents that paved the way for the 1954 Supreme Court decision that racially segregated elementary and secondary public schools were unconstitutional. This new constitutional interpretation swept away the longstanding "separate but equal" rationale mandating segregation in public facilities and radically changed the law of the land. Former NAACP/LDF director Jack Greenberg described the process as "erod[ing] . . . adverse precedent . . . in small steps."[20]

With the success of such early litigation campaigns in the background, public interest law groups in all fields try to maintain some degree of planning and control over their litigation activities, but these activities can be controlled only to a certain extent. Even Greenberg, in recalling the history of the NAACP/LDF antisegregation campaign, pointed to the "limits of planning."[21] "Mounting a litigation campaign is no easy task," one commentator explained in a recent article. "Not all litigation aimed at producing social change is 'planned' or takes the form of litigation campaigns. Nor are all test cases instances of planned litigation." In fact, much public interest litigation is guided by response to "fortuitous events."[22]

Today, public interest litigation is prompted by client groups, many of whom have developed sophisticated networks to inform lawyers about law suits to pursue. Cases may be referred from legal services organizations, sympathetic private attorneys, even from social workers or state or local agencies: for example, New York Lawyers for the Public Interest had a contract with the state of New York to handle developmental disability cases.[23]

Even for national public interest law organizations, potential cases increasingly tend to be referred by local lawyers and state officials and "whistleblowers." In some areas, there are active, if informal, networks of organizations that, in the words of Judith Lichtman of the Women's Legal Defense Fund, "talk to each other frequently and divide up the work."[24] Lichtman cites as an example the *Norris* case involving sex-based actuarial tables: the ACLU wrote an *amicus* Supreme Court brief, the National Women's Law Center made sure the local attorney had sufficient support, the Women's Legal Defense Fund lobbied the Equal Employment Opportunity Commission to maintain its sympathetic position, and the NOW Legal Defense Fund wrote a brief for members of Congress.

With potential cases coming in from a broad network of contacts rather than being internally generated, most organizations use some kind of formal screening process. In such a review, staff consider the relative merits of the case as well as such tactical questions as the availability of local resources, the costs involved, the reputation of the judge who would hear the case, publicity possibilities, and whether the potential plaintiff has access to other legal services. Most centers have litigation committees composed of staff, outside lawyers, and members of the organization's board of trustees, which must approve all litigation proposed by staff attorneys.

LITIGATION IN ACTION

Litigation in the public interest is important because the judiciary, unlike the other two branches of government, is relatively insulated from the direct influence of political interests. Federal judges and Supreme Court justices are appointed for life, and though some state judges serve elected terms, they generally do not have to be as concerned as other elected officials with filling the campaign war chest or political back-scratching. Nor are they as vulnerable to the influence of business interest groups as agency officials tend to be. The courts provide a forum in which the merits of an issue can speak more loudly than the power of the parties. In court, David may find himself on an equal footing with any financial or political Goliath.

In a 1963 opinion that vindicated the right of the NAACP to bring civil rights cases to court, Supreme Court Justice William Brennan stated that "litigation may well be the sole practicable avenue open to a minority to petition for redress of grievances."[25] Similarly, litigation is often the only means by which conflicts between citizens and powerful financial interests can be resolved. Although financial interests may all too often sway the executive and legislative branches, the courts are not for sale.

This is not to suggest that judges are not influenced by political perceptions or public attitudes. The tendency of judges to allow their political views to influence their decisions became more commonplace in the Reagan Administration, as discussed in Chapter 1. Public interest lawyers across the country report encountering greater hostility to their claims and remedies from newly appointed judges. However, while other social advocacy channels may be used more often in the future, litigation will continue to be a critical tool of social change.

The kinds of results that public interest lawyers have obtained through court action can be grouped under four broad headings: enforcing the law, applying and interpreting the law, restructuring public institutions, and acting as a catalyst for social and political change.

Enforcing the Law

Much of public interest litigation aims simply to enforce existing laws. The vast bulk of environmental and consumer cases deal with day-to-day issues such as monitoring public health statutes, and even a substantial portion of civil rights litigation is of the watchdog variety: keeping businesses operating within the law, or trying to make federal and state regulatory agencies perform their functions. Unlike many kinds of complex cases (e.g., antitrust or securities), where litigation can result in near-prohibitive expenses, legal challenges are often the least costly way to accomplish this monitoring function.

The law enforcement function gained particular importance in the deregulatory era of the Reagan Administration. Many agencies underwent personnel reductions which produced tremendous backlogs of complaints and greatly undermined their ability to carry out timely enforcement actions. In the environmental field, says the Sierra Club Legal Defense Fund's Sutherland, the recalcitrance of the executive agencies threatened to undercut completely the progress made by legislatures and the courts. "Without public interest lawyers representing concerned citizens willing to go to court, [the] strong environmental pronouncement [of the legislatures and courts] would have been rendered virtually meaningless. In fact, this is perhaps the most important role of environmental litigation—to compel government agencies and officials charged with administering our environmental laws to do their jobs."[26]

Under such circumstances, public interest lawyers' monitoring of the administrative agencies has become the last line of defense in citizen efforts to ensure that agency officials enforce regulations according to their legal obligations. Often, groups are forced to litigate to defend legislation whose passage they themselves were instrumental in securing. "There are statutory duties that represent values we are here to protect," stated Jonathan Lash, formerly of the Natural Resources Defense Council. "To ignore these violations would be to allow the congressional action we worked so hard for to go for nought."[27] Even the states have joined with environmental groups to take action to force federal regulatory agencies to implement the law. For example, New York and several other states sued in federal district court in 1985 to require the EPA to enforce regulations limiting particle emissions from steel plants in an effort to reduce acid rain in the eastern part of the country.

Applying and Interpreting the Law

Another crucial role of litigation lies in the judiciary's power to apply and interpret the law. Enactments passed by Congress and other legislative bodies often take the form of broad policies, and it becomes the responsibility of the courts to interpret and apply the law within the confines of specific situations.

Indeed, in his book *The Litigious Society*, journalist Jethro Lieberman suggests that it is becoming more and more common for legislative bodies to "punt" to the courts when dealing with new or highly controversial areas of public policy.[28] For example, notes Lieberman, Congress in the early 1960s ducked the job of creating a national environmental policy, instead passing the National Environmental Protection Act, which mandated that before actions can be taken that might seriously affect the environment, the Environental Protection Agency must study possible effects. "We have had *ad hoc* environmental decisions because Congress has prescribed no substantive environmental policy . . . In the main, the litigation conforms to the policy that Congress did lay down: to stop and think about the consequences of action before it is undertaken."[29]

Judicial decisions cumulatively build up the "detailed content" of legislation.[30] The role of public interest litigation in getting the courts to spell out the details of legislation has been particularly crucial in emerging areas of public policy: the Environmental Protection Act, the Occupational Safety and Health Act, and a large body of civil rights legislation.

Judicial review of the constitutionality of existing law tends to be the most visible and dramatic illustration of the courts' interpretive function. In these cases, the Supreme Court interprets the Constitution and sometimes articulates constitutional norms. The Supreme Court's decision in the *Brown* case that it was unconstitutional to exclude a black child from attending an all-white Topeka elementary school paved the way for an era of great extensions of civil rights through constitutional interpretation.

Some of the actions taken by courts to protect the rights of minorities have proved controversial, and critics have suggested that the involvement of the courts in such social issues has been too extensive. The fact remains, however, that among democratic institutions, the courts alone have as their central role the protection of individual rights. The elected legislative and executive branches of government are by their nature chiefly responsive to the will of the majority. When conflicts arise between the desires of the majority and the rights of a minority, the courts become the sole avenue of redress available to a legitimate minority interest. As U.S. Court of Appeals Judge Frank M. Johnson has stated, "once a constitutional deprivation has been shown, it becomes the duty of the court to render a decree which will as far as possible eliminate the effect of the past deprivations as well as bar like deprivations in the future."[31]

Restructuring Public Institutions

Affirmative decrees that courts have issued at the behest of citizen groups have often focused on changing such public institutions as schools, prisons, hospitals, and asylums. Such decrees may contain extensive and detailed instructions to the institution. Judges have been willing to use the full power of the courts—contempt citations, discovery actions, fines, the appointment of special masters, and a range of other remedies—to gain the compliance of public institutions and public officials.

Such affirmative decrees have been, in Professor Abram Chayes's words, "the centerpiece of the emerging public interest law model."[32] In 1972, for example, responding to evidence of unhealthy and dangerous conditions in state mental hospitals, a federal district judge in Alabama "issued a sweeping decree containing more than fifty specific mandatory changes in policy, plans, and operation of three state-run mental hospitals."[33] Judges have ordered states to establish individual treatment plans for mentally handicapped people previously "warehoused" in state facilities, insisting that steps be taken to place these people in the least restrictive practicable environment. In response to lawsuits demonstrating "barbarous" and dangerous prison conditions, judges mandated an end to the practice of placing two inmates in cells designed for one, forbade prisons from accepting any new prisoners until crowding was abated, and ordered a variety of other changes. So many of these suits were brought that in 1982 twenty-nine states were operating either individual institutions or entire prison systems under orders from federal judges.[34]

A Catalyst for Social Change

In spite of the ability of courts to promulgate affirmative decrees, the power of the courts to implement and enforce those decrees is relatively limited. The judiciary, after all, lacks both the financial power of the legislature and the police power of the executive. However, the courts can "serve as a publicist for reform in areas of the most pressing need," often encouraging other branches of government to take needed actions.[35] For example, Judge Johnson's decision concerning Alabama's mental institutions made it politically feasible for the state legislature not only to restore funding for the State Department of Mental Health, but to boost it above prior levels.[36] In a similar instance, litigation arising from a 1972 prisoner's lawsuit resulted in the State of Texas signing an agreement in 1985 that was "widely regarded as a landmark in Texas prison history," a blueprint for prison reform that reflected a "dramatic reversal in thinking on the part of the state's political and penal leadership."[37]

A Catalyst in the Legislative Process

Public interest litigation complements the legislative process in several ways. Judicial decisions that follow the passage of new legislation often serve to interpret its provisions. Even when unsuccessful, a public interest case may dramatize and publicize loopholes or injustices in existing law, thus spurring legislators to rethink public policy and pass new legislation to address the needs raised in trial.

The evolution of the Voting Rights Act of 1975 illustrates this process. In 1982, a major civil rights case, *City of Mobile v. Bolton*, contested Alabama's election system as discriminatory and therefore illegal. The trial court upheld the claim of discrimination and the Court of Appeals affirmed the decision, but the Supreme Court reversed it. The justices argued that, in order to prevail, the civil rights plaintiffs would have had to prove an intent to discriminate under Section II of the Voting Rights Act of 1965. As a direct result of this ruling, Congress clarified its policy in its reauthorization of the Voting Rights Act in 1982, stating that both intentional and *de facto* voting discrimination were illegal.

A similar process led to the passage of the Pregnancy Discrimination Act in 1982. A large coalition of women's labor, civil rights, and abortion groups joined together to persuade Congress to pass a bill reversing the Supreme Court's decision in *General Electric v. Gilbert* that had denied pregnant women the same protections guaranteed other working women under Title VII of the Civil Rights Act of 1964. As David Cohen, Co-Director of the Advocacy Institute, observed, "litigation informs the Congress of what the policy ought to be."[38]

A Catalyst for Public Education

Public interest court cases not only raise social issues, they also bring out the facts involved and stimulate public debate involving all concerned parties. Through discovery proceedings, public interest lawyers can obtain information that the ordinary citizen would have great difficulty in procuring, including on-the-record interviews with public officials, relevant documents of public agencies, and records of actions taken by participants. Many times, the expertise of public interest groups reveals obscure facts.

Bringing hidden conditions to light was crucial in the three-year court case in which the New York Civil Liberties Union and the Mental Health Law Project struggled to improve conditions in Willowbrook State School, a scandal-ridden institution for the mentally retarded. Courtroom evidence of neglect, injuries, and even deaths in this home for mentally retarded children and adults sufficiently aroused public consciousness to cause state officials to work toward a consent decree to ameliorate conditions for residents. The well-publicized case also educated the public about the rights of retarded people to as normal a life as possible and about the importance of providing care in smaller, community-based facilities.

The petition brought before the Nuclear Regulatory Commission by Ellyn Weiss for the Union of Concerned Scientists significantly increased public awareness. In 1977, six months after the Three Mile Island incident, the petition focused public attention on the inadequacies of the evacuation plan for communities around the Indian Point Nuclear Power Plant in New York. It pointed out that Indian Point was within fifty miles of New York City, a location chosen in the 1950s, before citing standards were written, and at a time when "the implicit assumption was that there would be no nuclear power plant accidents," recalls Weiss.[39] The New York Public Interest Research Group joined the case, contacting local groups and public officials. A total of 150 witnesses—local government officials, police, school officials, and citizen groups—testified at the hearing, an unprecedented number for the Nuclear Regulatory Commission. Although the petition failed in its attempt to shut down the Indian Point plant, better emergency planning procedures were adopted, and community consciousness of nuclear safety issues was raised.

Another example of the public education role of litigation involved the New York Lawyers for the Public Interest's (NYLPI) successful case to restore the jobs of ten mentally disabled Postal Service workers. Employees of ten years' standing, they were fired when the managers who had hired them were replaced by new supervisors. NYLPI sued, the cases were settled out of court, and the postal workers were rehired. According to former director Jean Murphy, NYLPI took full advantage of the public education aspects of the case, making it into "an opportunity to do some consciousness-raising about disabled people" with both union and Equal Employment Opportunity Commission officials.[40]

Public interest litigation in one area can also produce important ripple effects in other areas of public policy. For example, lawsuits that successfully challenged prison conditions paved the way for similar cases against mental institutions.

In summing up the gains of recent prison litigation, Adjoa Aiyetoro, staff attorney at the National Prison Project, emphasized the role of litigation as a catalyst for larger social change. Litigation, said Aiyetoro, has "established that prisons are not exempt from the rule of law," legitimized the issues of prisoners and institutions, changed prison conditions, caused more alternative programs to be established, and encouraged the corrections establishment to "clean up [its] own house" and develop professional standards.[41]

CRITICISMS OF LITIGATION

Because of the impressive record of fostering social progress in many areas of public policy, public interest litigation has generated criticism. Indeed, the very successes of public interest lawyers have aroused the hostility of losing defendants and their allies. Some critics complain that the courts have played too activist a role and blame public interest lawyers for this development. Such criticisms include claims that: public interest cases slow down the processes of government and clog an already overburdened court system; the judiciary lacks the legitimacy and competence necessary to set social policy; and public interest law organizations are narrowly focused on abstract policy issues in Washington, D.C., rather than on grassroots issues of community empowerment. This section will explain why such criticisms lack validity.

Many people sympathetic to the public interest law movement have expressed dismay about the mushrooming expense of litigation, the growing sophistication of defendants, the increasing complexity of the legal environment, and the ephemeral quality of some court victories. Others have been concerned because litigation upsets powerful interests (especially in environmental cases where major economic interests may be at stake), and because some remedial court decrees (for example, court-ordered busing) have antagonized vocal segments of the general population as well. They have wondered if the traditionally adversarial relationships of the courtroom are conducive to finding appropriate remedies when different legitimate public interests compete.[42]

Practical and Financial Concerns

Taking major public interest cases to court is costly and growing more so. Indeed, it is difficult to predict the total costs of a case at the outset. The NAACP Legal Defense and Education Fund has found that the costs of civil rights cases, which involve a great deal of fact finding and discovery, have tripled over the past five years. To litigate an average employment discrimination case cost $65,000.[43] The price of litigation, however, can go much higher: the costs of one Kansas desegregation case rose to $800,000.[44]

Part of the reason that costs are escalating is that, as the most blatant forms of discrimination are successfully challenged in the courts, new cases tend to deal with subtler forms which are more complex and difficult to litigate. Experts such as statisticians are needed in employment, voting rights, and other types of civil rights cases. People with specialized research skills are needed to bring a case and to assist lawyers in preparing testimony. Another important factor has been the greater sophistication of government, corporations, and other defendants. Increasingly, public interest lawyers challenge defendants who are bolstered by their own sets of social statistics, their own testimony from expert witnesses, and scholarly theories favorable to their own positions—tactics they have learned from public interest lawyers.

Environmental groups, in particular, have come up against the elaborate "cost-benefit" computer analyses that the Environmental Protection Agency has been using to rationalize its lack of enforcement actions in, for example, the regulation of airborne toxins. Regardless of the merits of a case, government and corporate defendants in general tend to have more resources than do public interest groups to develop such sophisticated forms of evidence.

In litigation, the focus of the court proceeding frequently shifts from whether something should be done to address the grievance of the plaintiff to more complex questions of what remedies might be appropriate or what compensation would be adequate for an entire class of people affected. However, working out such an affirmative decree may be time-consuming and complex. As one federal district court judge described the process: "In addition to advice from experts, the parties, intervenors, and *amici* are invited to submit their recommendations and suggestions, usually in the form of proposed plans."[45] At this point, all the intellectual resources of the network of the public interest plaintiff may be called into play to contribute to the devising of an appropriate remedy. This network of concerned citizens and organizations may also be involved in monitoring the implementation of the court-ordered remedy, often involving costly efforts stretching far into the future.

Of course, not all public interest litigation is complex or expensive. In some situations, it can be extremely cost-effective and lead to a quick resolution. In 1982, the Food Research and Action Center (FRAC) and several states sued the federal government to expedite funding for the Women, Infants, and Children (WIC) program through the federal-state-local "pipeline." Relief came almost immediately. As former FRAC director Nancy Amidei recalls, "On Tuesday, FRAC went to court, USDA was ordered to do a survey of funds, and on the following Tuesday, funds were going out."[46] FRAC had spent very little money on litigation and achieved a large programmatic remedy in return.

Some critics of public interest litigation say that it is too narrowly focused on policy abstractions, and not sufficiently involved in grass-roots issues of community empowerment. However, public interest law provides citizens with the tools to control and improve their own lives: to limit air and water pollution, to ensure access to the workplace for women and minorities, and to open public accommodations to the disabled. Gains such as these enable individuals and communities to exercise their full rights as citizens.

Perhaps the greatest frustration of litigation for those who practice public interest law is that "individual victories require constant monitoring so that they don't become paper victories" resulting in very little change. "I never expected it would take so long to implement court decisions," admits Alvin Bronstein, citing a 1977 case in which the Rhode Island maximum security institution was ordered closed, yet still remains open today.[47] The difficulties experienced by the Prison Project in persuading courts to issue remedial orders, particularly when the public is hostile or apathethic, extend to the entire civil rights community. "It often seems like you never win," comments Judith Lichtman. "Your adversaries keep coming back. You have to constantly fight to win battles you thought were over."[48]

Advocates for deinstitutionalization have witnessed an even more ironic turn of events. The movement achieved great legal victories in obtaining the release of many mental patients from prison-like institutions. However, lacking the establishment of sufficient community-based care facilities, many former mental patients may go untreated and experience severe relapses, often ending up destitute and homeless. As Norman Rosenberg, Executive Director of the Mental Health Law Project, states, "the public interest movement played a major role in the deinstitutionalization struggle, in getting people out of institutions who didn't need to be there. This struggle has been largely won. But the struggle to establish adequate community-based services, such as community residential facilities, case management services, sheltered workshops, job training programs, and crisis services is still going on."[49] These newer issues, in some ways more subtle and complex than the old deinstitutionalization issues, are taxing much of the efforts of underfunded mental health advocates today, according to Rosenberg.

Although litigation can be expensive and complex, and sometimes achieving the desired goal can be elusive, taking a case to court may often be the best, or indeed the only tactic available. Frequently there is no alternative to litigation if progress is to be made, or if gains made in the past are to be defended.

Controversial Consequences

Some of the court decisions arising from public interest litigation have been extremely controversial, even leading to vehement public protest. As Jethro Lieberman notes:

> In many cases, judicial intervention into the realm of public policy has prompted street demonstrations, aggravated the tendency toward single-interest politics with all its distortions of the political process, and created several serious attempts, so far none successful, to amend the Constitution (for example, to deal with busing, reapportionment, and abortion). The reason for public hostility is not far to seek: in almost every case in which they have declared a constitutional right, the courts have acted contrary to the discernible wishes of a majority of the people.[50]

However, as Lieberman is quick to point out, "majority disapproval is scarcely conclusive."[51] Much public interest litigation is by nature controversial. But controversial actions can be crucially important ones. The *Brown* decision was widely denounced by social scientists as well as editorial writers, remembers Jack Greenberg, former Director of the NAACP/LDF.[52] On the capital punishment issues, where the NAACP/LDF has lost ground in recent years, the majority of the public is hostile to the position that capital punishment should be outlawed.

Not every public interest law suit may be well advised, nor may every affirmative judicial decree formulated by judges turn out to be efficacious. Even so, says Greenberg, "you have to strike a balance, and with each case, judge whether the net effect will be better than if the case had not been brought. It's always a judgment call." Achieving results is costly and may produce a backlash, but Greenberg believes that "on balance these cases are bringing about greater equity."[53]

Legitimacy and Competence Fears

The procedural rulings that broadened access to parties wishing to bring grievances to the courts, the spread of public interest law activity to most major policy areas, and the resulting increased involvement of the courts in working out public policy have all raised questions, especially among conservatives, about the legitimacy and competence of the judiciary to play this augmented role. Are the courts really an appropriate forum to settle complex social issues? Are judges really competent to decide how a mental hospital should be run, how police officers should treat those arrested for crimes, or by what formula a community should assign its children to the public schools?

Some people have worried that the activities of public interest lawyers have tipped the constitutional balance of powers away from the legislative and executive branches of government too far towards the judicial branch. Judicial activism, some fear, has become judicial overreaching—in Nathan Glazer's phrase, the courts are becoming an "imperial judiciary," usurping the legitimate role of elected government.[54] Others have been concerned about the competence of judges to formulate public policy.

These arguments manifest a lack of understanding about the role of the judiciary. It is an established principle that the courts' unique function is the preservation of individual rights. As articulated by Chief Justice Marshall in the landmark Supreme Court opinion, *Marbury v. Madison*, the power of the federal judiciary lies in the protection it affords constitutional rights of minority groups and individuals against unjust or discriminatory government action.[55]

In addition, some statutes, such as the Clean Water and Air Acts, give the courts jurisdiction to hear citizen enforcement lawsuits. Through these statutes Congress specifically calls upon the judiciary to define the duties and responsibilities of the federal government and individuals in handling environmental issues.

To some extent, protests by Glazer and others may be moot. President Reagan's appointment of a large number of judges who favor judicial restraint has meant that courts have become more cautious. Claims to adequate health care, education, and public services rarely receive protection in the federal courts. Additionally, the judiciary over the past several years has steadily limited access to the courts by the poor, consumers, and civil rights plaintiffs and restricted available remedies for persons who have been deprived of the benefits of federal statutes. For example, courts have imposed several technical and burdensome requirements which make it more difficult for plaintiffs to get their cases into court.

Another argument raised by critics of public interest law is that the interests asserted by public interest plaintiffs are already adequately represented by the government, whose principal business is to regulate the market so that it operates safely. There are at least two flaws in this argument.

First, many of the actions taken by government are perceived by the public to threaten its health and safety. If private law suits are not permitted, there is no effective way of testing the legality of executive or legislative branch decisionmaking. Second, the well-documented history of the capture of government agencies by those they are charged with regulating suggests that many law suits would not be brought if the decision to litigate were left solely to the government.

Nonetheless, "the scholarly historical debate over the legitimacy of judicial review curiously goes on, although it is a debate about an accomplished fact."[56] The courts have been drawn into a public policy vacuum created by the reluctance or inability of the other two branches of government to set policy adequately. Further, the complex role of the judiciary today may not present as much of a challenge to the balance of powers between the different branches of government as some claim. "In practice, all governmental officials, including judges, have exercised a large and messy admixture of powers, and that is as it must be," writes Abram Chayes.[57] Affirmative decrees do not spring, full-blown, out of heads of judges like a mythical Minerva from the head of Jupiter. Rather, their content tends to be developed from precedent, evidence, and the recommendations of the parties to the case.

Many of the criticisms of public interest litigation—that lawyers represent no real client, that the cases should not be granted standing, that the issues may be frivolous—reveal a lack of appreciation of what public interest law is, how it operates, and what it can accomplish. Conservatives' concerns that public interest litigation inordinately slows down the processes of government, that it clogs the court system, or that the personal motives of public interest lawyers are not sufficiently pure seem disingenuous, masking what is more nearly a distaste for the results of successful public interest litigation. Much of public interest litigation is aimed at getting government to do what it is legally obliged to do, however much debate there may be as to the extent and nature of that obligation.

ALTERNATIVE DISPUTE RESOLUTION

Because of the inherent difficulties of litigation, some advocates have focused on alternative dispute resolution as a substitute. Indeed, mediation is, as environmental attorney Patrick A. Parenteau puts it, a useful "tool," and early experiments with it have been promising.[58] However, the experiences of many public interest advocates indicate that it is only likely to produce solid results in a relatively narrow set of circumstances in which the controversy involves negotiable issues, as opposed to non-negotiable matters of principle; the number of people at the table is relatively small; the interests of the principals have been defined and accepted as legitimate; the critical facts are known or knowable within reasonable cost and time constraints; there is a rough parity of power among parties (that is, if each party has some leverage over the others); and there is some pressure (for example, a statutory deadline) on everyone to reach an agreement in a timely fashion.

It is important to note here that in the public interest law arena, unlike many other areas of law, the question is often not negotiation *or* trial, but negotiation *in the context* of trial. In the typical public interest case,

> The traditional adversary relationship is suffused and intermingled with negotiating and mediating processes at every point. The judge is the dominant figure in organizing and guiding the case, and he draws for support not only on the parties and their counsel, but on a wide range of outsiders—masters, experts, and oversight personnel.[59]

Because of the escalating costs of litigation, out-of-court settlements are becoming more important. But there may also be a negative side to settlements. A compromise settlement can leave plaintiffs dissatisfied, with a sense that justice has not been done, and can sometimes disaffect them from a movement rather than increase their resolve to remain active advocates. On the other hand, organizations that have worked together on a court case often continue to cooperate to monitor implementation and to carry on additional advocacy activities. Litigation can be an effective organizing device, a vehicle for "setting in motion other political processes and for building coalitions and alliances."[60]

Public interest litigation, then, remains one of the most important of a variety of strategies—constituent/community organizing, public education, legislative and regulatory advocacy, monitoring of federal agencies—designed to help define the values of our society and to advance social change. In some cases, litigation may be an expedient tactic, a relatively inexpensive means of bringing about a desired end;

in others, the costs and difficulties may be enormous. But in any event, there will always be some cases that advocates must take to court simply because the judiciary is the only real avenue of redress.

Notes

1. Alliance for Justice interview with Norman Rosenberg, Executive Director, Mental Health Law Project, May 19, 1986.

2. Alliance for Justice interview with Armando Menocal, Staff Attorney, Public Advocates, Inc., May 22, 1986.

3. Address by Charles Halpern to the Alliance for Justice conference, "Preserving Access To Justice," June 10, 1985.

4. "The Coming of Age of the Public Interest Lobbyist." Address by Michael Pertschuk, former Federal Trade Commissioner, to the Political Science Forum, March 21, 1984.

5. Alliance for Justice interview with Burton Fretz, Executive Director, National Senior Citizens Law Center, July 20, 1984.

6. Alliance for Justice interview with Norman Dean, former General Counsel, National Wildlife Federation, September 20, 1985.

7. "Looking Ahead: The Future of Public Interest Law." Address by Ralph Nader to the Alliance for Justice conference, "Preserving Access to Justice," June 11, 1985.

8. Alliance interview with Rosenberg, May 19, 1986.

9. Carlyle Hall, Jr., "Public Interest By the Numbers," 31 *Stanford Law Review* (May 1979), p. 989.

10. Alliance for Justice interview with Judith Lichtman, Executive Director, Women's Legal Defense Fund, March 4, 1988.

11. Alliance for Justice interview with Robert Schwartz, Executive Director, Juvenile Law Center, September 28, 1984.

12. Neil Goldschmidt, former U. S. Secretary of Transportation, as quoted in *Center for Law in the Public Interest Profile*, September 1984, p. 3.

13. Alliance for Justice interview with Norman Rosenberg, Executive Director, Mental Health Law Project, March 4, 1986.

14. Alliance for Justice interview with Peter Forsythe, Vice President, Edna McConnell Clark Foundation, July 2, 1984.

15. Alliance for Justice interview with Nancy Amidei, former Executive Director, Food Research and Action Center, February 14, 1984.

16. Alliance for Justice interview with environmental lawyer Richard Mallory, May 3, 1985.

17. Address by Frederic P. Sutherland, Executive Director, Sierra Club Legal Defense Fund, to the National Affairs and Legislation and Conservation Committees of the Garden Club of America, October 8, 1984.

18. Arthur S. Flemming, as cited in Penny Chorlton, "Groups to Monitor 'Regressive' Rights Actions," *Washington Post*, July 20, 1982, p. A15.

19. "Litigation as a Tool of Empowerment for the Poor." Address by William L. Taylor to the National Neighborhood Coalition Conference, November 25, 1985.

20. Presentation by Jack Greenberg of the thirtieth annual Benjamin N. Cardozo Lecture, "Litigation for Social Change: Methods, Limits and Role in Democracy." Delivered before the Association of the Bar of New York, October 31, 1973.

21. *Ibid.*

22. Stephen L. Wasby, "Civil Rights Litigation by Organizations: Contraints and Choices," 68 *Judicature* 9–10 (April–May 1985), pp. 338, 343.

23. Alliance for Justice interview with Jean Murphy, former Executive Director, New York Lawyers for the Public Interest, July 3, 1984.

24. Alliance interview with Lichtman, February 9, 1984.

25. *NAACP v. Button*, 371 U.S. 415, 429–31 (1963).

26. Address by Sutherland to the Garden Club, October 8, 1984.

27. Jonathan Lash, as quoted in Lawrence Mosher, "Environmentalists Sue to Put an End to 'Regulatory Massive Resistance,'" 13 *National Journal* 4 (December 19, 1981), p. 2223.

28. Jethro K. Lieberman, *The Litigious Society*. (New York: Basic Books, 1981), p. 98.

29. *Ibid.*, p. 108.

30. James Willard, "The Function of the Courts in the United States, 1950–1980," 15 *Law & Society Review* 3–41 (1980–1981), p. 453.

31. Frank M. Johnston, Jr., "Thinking About the Federal Judiciary," *New York Times*, April 9, 1977, p. C15.

32. Abram Chayes, "The Role of the Judge in Public Law Litigation," 89 *Harvard Law Review* 7 (May 1976), p. 1298.

33. Lieberman, *Litigious Society*, p. 115.

34. Wendell Rawls, Jr., "Judges' Authority in Prison Reform Attacked," *New York Times*, May 18, 1982, p. A1.

35. Lieberman, *Litigious Society*, p. 128.

36. *Ibid.*

37. Robert Reinhold, "Texas Reaches Accord to End Prison Dispute," *New York Times*, July 5, 1985, p. A14.

38. Alliance interview David Cohen, Co-Director, Advocacy Institute, December 3, 1983.

39. Alliance for Justice interview with Ellyn Weiss, partner, Harmon and Weiss, April 17, 1984.

40. Alliance interview with Murphy, July 3, 1984.

41. Alliance for Justice interview with Adjoa Aiyetoro, staff attorney, National Prison Project, December 22, 1983.

42. *Public Interest Law: Five Years Later.* A report by the Ford Foundation and the American Bar Association Special Committee on Public Interest Practice (March 1976), p. 30.

43. Alliance for Justice interview with Barry Goldstein, Staff Attorney, NAACP Legal Defense and Education Fund, April 13, 1987.

44. Alliance for Justice interview with Jean Fairfax, Staff Attorney, NAACP Legal Defense and Education Fund, July 3, 1984.

45. Johnston, "Thinking About the Federal Judiciary."

46. Alliance interview with Amidei, February 14, 1984.

47. Alliance interview with Bronstein, December 22, 1983.

48. Alliance interview with Lichtman, February 9, 1984.

49. Alliance for Justice interview with Norman Rosenberg, Executive Director, Mental Health Law Project, November 1, 1985.

50. Lieberman, *Litigious Society,* p. 113.

51. *Ibid.,* p. 114.

52. Alliance for Justice interview with Jack Greenberg, former Director, NAACP Legal Defense and Education Fund, July 3, 1984.

53. *Ibid.*

54. Nathan Glazer, "Toward an Imperial Judiciary?" *The Public Interest,* vol. 41 (Fall 1975), p. 118.

55. *United States v. Richardson,* 418 US 166, 694 (1974).

56. Greenberg address, "Litigation for Social Change."

57. Chayes, "Role of the Judge," p. 1307.

58. Patrick A. Parenteau, "An Environmentalist Perspective on Mediation vs. Litigation." Address to the American Law Institute—American Bar Association Conference on Environmental Law, February 24, 1984.

59. Chayes, "Role of the Judge," p. 1284.

60. Gary Bellow, "The New Public Interest Lawyers," 79 *Yale Law Journal* 970 (1970), p. 1087.

6

Widening Influence and Maturation
of Public Interest Law

*One thing that the Reagan Administration has helped to make clearer is the
fact that long-distance runners are the kinds of people that are needed for
the kind of adventure we've undertaken.*[1]

*Public interest law, one industry lobbyist says with resignation, "is a part
of the scene today, and that's just the way it is."*[2]

"It used to be that a story about product recall would get on the
front page of the daily paper. Now, you see this kind of story on page
40."[3] To an extent, Ralph Nader's remark was perhaps a protest against
the complacency of the media regarding consumer protection issues.
But the comment also testifies to a widespread acceptance today of
the once controversial idea of compelling a company to call back a
product deemed dangerous to consumers. The fact that such recalls
are no longer the big news they were when public interest advocates
such as Ralph Nader started out is not simply due to the public's
familiarity with the idea; it is also attributable to consumer groups
who have established product recall as a viable option for regulatory
authorities and manufacturers. Because of these efforts, laws now exist
requiring manufacturers to place serial numbers, warning labels, and
other descriptive data on products. Other reforms allow consumer
advocates and the media to publicize the manufacturers and brand
names of dangerous products without fear of retaliatory law suits.

PART OF THE MAINSTREAM

As with product recall, many other ideas introduced through public
interest advocacy have become institutional norms. Basic value choices—
that the workplace be free from hazards, that the air and water be
clean, that products be safe and reliable—are raised by advocates in

Congress, the courts, federal and state agencies, and state legislatures around the country.

Public interest advocates have won landmark court decisions. Minorities and the politically powerless have secured greater protections through the courts. Freedom of Information and Administrative Procedure Act lawsuits have opened rulemaking processes to public scrutiny and enabled citizens to participate in agency decisionmaking.

Through the leadership of public interest lawyers, a large number of attorneys in private practice take on *pro bono* public interest work. The movement can take a large share of the credit for the fact that most law schools now provide some form of clinical legal education and that many offer specialized training in public interest law. It can also take credit for institutionalizing the use of legal advocacy, a strategy now commonly employed by a wide range of charitable, educational, cultural, community, and service organizations. Indeed, the fact that the conservative movement has adopted the tactics of public interest lawyers is a real testament to the latter's effectiveness.

The public's continued support of the goals of environmental and consumer protection groups is another indication of public interest law's place in the mainstream. A 1967 Louis Harris poll noted that the public opposed—by 46 percent to 44 percent—paying $15 more in federal taxes to finance efforts to clean up the air and water. But by 1971, "Americans listed pollution control as a national problem second only to the state of the economy."[4] In 1982, a Roper Organization survey reported that 69 percent of Americans approved of environmental laws and regulations or thought they were not stringent enough, while only 21 percent thought they had gone too far.[5] Similar surveys show that large majorities support regulations that strengthen consumer rights and remedies: "When the regulation means the government stepping in to protect small companies against ruinous price cutting by larger rivals, or protecting individual consumers against the rapacious price-gouging or shoddy products of corporations, people are all for it."[6]

Through advocacy and public education, public interest lawyers have also armed voters with facts and information to elect politicians committed to consumer and environmental protection. Although centers are prohibited by law from becoming involved in political campaigns, they raise issues around which citizens' groups, without similar restrictions, often mobilize. Nor has the ban on political activity diminished groups' influence with politicians themselves. A recent *New York Times* article reports that one candidate who is making a bid for the 1988 Democratic presidential nomination is "taking steps to resolve longstanding differences with [environmental organizations] over his environmental policies."[7]

Just as the goals and tactics of public interest law have gained currency and acceptance, so have public interest lawyers themselves become less controversial. The former zealots have watched their causes become careers as their groups become well-established, influential organizations. They are widely recognized as experts in their fields and are often invited to serve on special commissions and task forces. The events they sponsor serve as forums for prominent leaders in Congress, government, and the nonprofit community to present their ideas on current issues and strategies.

COMING OF AGE

Operating in an arena that is by definition contentious, public interest advocates will always be involved in confrontational situations. But their style and tactics have changed with the times and matured with their greater influence. Environmental advocates, for example, prefer "out-researching and out-negotiating a corporate leader, not damning him in public," presenting themselves as "problem solvers, not screamers." Their organizations are "a cut more managerial and less confrontational than their predecessors," and they have attempted to form "closer alliances with farmers [on issues such as soil conservation], with labor [on toxic wastes] and with corporations that believe fair and consistent environmental regulation is in their long-term interest."[8]

Although the number of attorneys who practice public interest law full-time is relatively small, the community also includes a great body of able and interested lawyers all over the country who can be tapped to act as cooperating attorneys. The Sierra Club Legal Defense Fund, for example, is in contact with lawyers in every part of the country. The NAACP Legal Defense and Education Fund (NAACP/LDF) works on civil rights with 400 cooperating attorneys from thirty-four states.[9]

Public interest organizations increasingly are being recognized for their contributions. In 1983, the Natural Resources Defense Council won Long Island University's George Polk Award for Special Interest Publications with its *Amicus* magazine. It also received an award from the U.S. Attorney General in March 1979 for having "materially contributed to the attainment of the highest standards of law enforcement and justice."

Public interest lawyers have become widely recognized spokespersons for their causes. Their organizations have acquired reputations for achieving results, which enables them to apply pressure in other situations. "One of the reasons our firm can succeed," says Armando

Menocal of Public Advocates, Inc., "is that, in addition to being innovative, we've achieved a rather substantial track record."[10] This institutional weight allows groups to bargain with industry and goverment officials on an equal footing.

The coming of age of public interest lawyers and citizens' groups sometimes can mean that constituencies and causes conflict with each other. In Alaska, for instance, Native Americans have pushed for sovereignty over lands they assert belongs to their tribe. Environmental groups, on the other hand, have sometimes opposed these efforts on the basis that the land should be subject to state and federal control.[11] Job seniority versus affirmative action considerations is another issue which can divide public interest groups into two camps.

In addition, public interest law firms, both private and nonprofit, have become training grounds for a new generation of local elected officials and judges. Henry Marsh, former mayor of Richmond, Virginia, was a cooperating attorney with the NAACP/LDF. Judge Patricia Wald of the U.S. Court of Appeals for the District of Columbia Circuit was an attorney with the Mental Health Law Project, and Oscar Adams, the first black judge on the Alabama Supreme Court, was also an NAACP/LDF cooperating attorney. Others have gone into policy-making roles in government. Ross Sandler, for example, formerly with the Natural Resources Defense Council, went on to become the Commissioner of the New York Department of Transportation.

Finally, public interest lawyers in other countries, inspired by the progress made by environmental, civil rights, and consumer attorneys in the United States, have founded public interest offices in South Africa, India, and Israel, among other places. The Legal Resource Center, established in Johannesburg in 1979, has "helped ease some of the harsh features of [South Africa's] apartheid regime."[12] Funded by the Ford and Carnegie Foundations and the Rockefeller Brothers Fund, it has expanded its staff from two to seventeen lawyers, and its supporters now include organizations and individuals throughout South Africa and in Europe. The Association for Civil Rights in Israel, developed by Professor Herman Schwartz of the Washington College of Law, provides two-year fellowships to Israeli lawyers. A fellow spends the first year in Washington, D.C., studying at American University and interning at a civil liberties organization. For the second year, the fellowship pays for the intern's salary to work full-time at an Israeli civil rights group.[13]

A LASTING LEGACY

Clinical legal education is one of the enduring legacies of the public interest law movement. Prior to the late 1960s, such hands-on exposure to case work was almost unheard of at law schools. Seed grants from the Ford Foundation's Council for Legal Education for Professional Responsibility encouraged the development of clinical programs, and, although still controversial among some segments of the academic community, they have caught on. In 1984 the American Bar Association reported that 169 of 173 accredited law schools had incorporated some form of clinical education into their overall programs. Spearheading the movement were centers such as Georgetown's Institute for Public Representation (IPR) and Rutgers' Constitutional Litigation Clinic, Urban Legal Clinic, and Women's Rights Clinic. IPR is unique in serving both as a clinical education program and a public interest law firm. In addition to three senior attorneys, its staff includes five graduate fellows who supervise fifteen law students each semester.

Most clinics are modeled after the legal services prototype, providing low-cost legal assistance to clients who could not otherwise afford it. Increasingly, they are expanding their focus to include law reform litigation as well. The best of these programs offer the student the opportunity to "work with real clients, on real legal matters, and have real responsibility—under supervision—for a case as a whole," believes Elliot Milstein, Director of Clinical Programs at the Washington College of Law's Practicing Law Center. Milstein estimates that perhaps 60 percent of law schools have clinical programs that meet these requirements.[14]

One innovative new law school, the City University of New York at Queens College, has adopted the clinical model for its entire curriculum. Launched in 1984 by Charles Halpern, and now directed by Haywood Burns, the school is devoted to training lawyers to work for public interest organizations and governmental agencies, rather than for corporate law firms. While providing students with the necessary groundwork in legal doctrine and theory, the interdisciplinary curriculum stresses practical skills such as client contact, legal research, and trial procedure, and exposes students to the historical, social, and philosophical contexts of public interest law. Students tend to be older than average, and many come to the school with substantial experience in public service work. About half are women and more than one-fourth are minorities.

INSTITUTIONALIZATION AND MATURATION

Although still accounting for only a small proportion of total legal activity, public interest law has, to a significant degree, been institutionalized in the American legal system. As a result of the efforts of public interest lawyers, constitutional norms have been established, and an important body of law has been promulgated, ranging from civil rights to environmental and consumer protections. These reforms have helped produce a society that, although certainly not perfect, is far more just and fair for citizens than the society of the past. A broad range of public interest legal centers have been established and have survived harsh turns in the political climate. As one commentator remarked about the Chicago-based Business and Professional People for the Public Interest (BPI),

> Most of the other activist troops spawned in the late '60s have gone straight. Rennie Davis is selling insurance. Tom Hayden is a politician. Eldridge Cleaver has found religion, and Joan Baez has finally denounced Hanoi. But BPI is still kicking, celebrating its 10th birthday.[15]

The network of sympathetic private attorneys who may be tapped to work on specific cases stretches far beyond the group of lawyers who practice public interest law on a full-time basis. Law schools have incorporated the clinical approach in their curricula, and many offer specialized training in public interest law.

Finally, the public interest law movement is responsible for the widespread public recognition of the importance of legal advocacy. The idea of working to ensure that all segments of society enjoy their legally mandated rights and protections was not a common one before the 1960s. Today, many charitable groups, membership organizations, and goverment agencies consider legal advocacy to be one of their core functions, and it has become an indispensable technique in most citizen efforts toward social betterment. Public interest law has become a recognized, important, and permanent feature of the American legal landscape.

Notes

1. Address by Charles Halpern to the Alliance for Justice conference, "Preserving Access to Justice," June 10, 1985.

2. As quoted in Fred Strasser, "Public Interest Law Acquires the Concerns of Middle Age," *National Law Journal*, vol. 7, no. 22 (February 11, 1985), p. 1.

3. Ralph Nader, interviewed by John Goldsmith on "Capital Edition," WUSA-TV Channel 9 (CBS), November 2, 1985, 10:30 a.m.

4. William Symonds, "The Grip of the Green Giant," *Fortune Magazine*, vol. 106 (October 4, 1982), p. 138.

5. *Ibid.*, p. 140.

6. *National Law Journal Opinion Outlook Briefing Paper*, vol. 1, no. 19 (August 24, 1981) (Washington, D.C.: Government Research Corporation, 1981), p. 2.

7. "Dukakis Shift Seen on Environment," *New York Times* (March 1, 1987), p. 46.

8. Neal R. Pierce, "Environmental Activists Taking a New Tack," 17 *National Journal* 3 (August 3, 1985), p. 1808.

9. Alliance interview with Charles Stephen Ralston, First Assistant Council, NAACP Legal Defense and Education Fund, June 9, 1986.

10. Armando Menocal, as quoted in Martin Baron, "Public Advocates: Small Law Firm Keeps Beating the Corporate Giants," *Los Angeles Times* (October 7, 1980), p. 6.

11. Alliance for Justice interviews with Durwood Zaelke, Senior Staff Attorney, Sierra Club Legal Defense Fund, and Henry Sockbeson, Staff Attorney, Native American Rights Fund, April 3, 1987.

12. David Margolick, "Civil Bar Association Hails A Legal Foe of Apartheid," *New York Times* (March 25, 1985), p. 2.

13. Alliance for Justice interview with Professor Herman Schwartz, Washington College of Law of the American University, January 4, 1985.

14. Alliance for Justice interview with Elliot Milstein, Director of Clinical Programs, Practicing Law Center, Washington College of Law, May 19, 1986.

15. Civia Tamarkin, "The White Knights of BPI," *Chicago Tribune Magazine* (November 25, 1979), Sect. 9, pp. 82–85.

7

Conclusions and Recommendations

But what do we want to do in terms of broadening the vistas and the options for public interest advocacy? First of all, is it still attractive to the young? That's always the litmus test. Secondly, we've got to deal with new mechanisms of organizations, to build more institutions.[1]

Public interest law has demonstrated its worth in the American legal system, making major contributions in realizing the rights of minorities, women, and disadvantaged groups, protecting consumers and the environment, and ensuring the civil liberties of the underrepresented. Nonetheless, the resources available to this field remain scarce. For example, it is estimated that, at a bare minimum, $391 million per year is needed for legal services for the poor.[2] The current federal budget, however, calls for substantially less than this amount. Furthermore, only about one tenth of one percent of total foundation funding and individual charitable contributions went to public interest law groups in 1983.

The contrast between the resources available to the private bar and those available to the public one is dramatic. Businesses can finance their legal expenses through tax deductions, and the private practice of law has never been more lucrative. Major law firms in cities such as New York and Washington, D.C. are paying starting salaries of $70,000, staffing their offices with more than sufficient support personnel, and researching cases with sophisticated, high-tech data bases. Highly credentialed and experienced lawyers devoting their careers to serving the public interest, on the other hand, accept significant personal and financial sacrifices, perform legal work with small, overstretched support staffs, and still must "shepardize" their cases.

Most of the readers of this book—members of the legal profession, law students and teachers, members of the philanthropic community, advocates in many fields, elected officials, appointed public servants, and public interest legal professionals themselves—have some understanding of the importance of public interest law. But American society, both the public and private sectors, needs to bolster its commitment to making it an enduring part of the legal system. The following recommendations are aimed at assisting in such an effort.

WHAT FOUNDATIONS CAN DO

Foundations have long been a mainstay of funding for public interest law. Foundations that have made substantial grants in the field should continue to do so, and other foundations should be encouraged to play an increasing role. Now that public interest groups are experiencing the dual crunch of both increased workloads and federal funding cuts, the philanthrophic community has a special responsibility to give the clientele served by legal groups and the groups themselves greater priority.

The importance of advocacy in helping to solve some of society's most severe problems was specifically noted by one prestigious foundation. In 1983, in response to federal budget cuts and economic recession, the Minneapolis Foundation convened a working group of community leaders to identify and evaluate solutions for emergency needs in Minnesota. Several counties were experiencing an unprecedented demand for food, housing, and employment, not only from the inner-city poor, but from the elderly, unemployed, and women with children. The report's recommendations in a number of different categories called for the development of advocacy programs to address particular problems.[3]

Philanthropy is a valuable tool for addressing public needs and eliminating national problems of poverty, injustice, and racism and the malfunctioning of government and corporate institutions. However, according to Elizabeth McCormack, Vice-President of the J.D.R. 3rd Fund and Director of the John D. and Catherine T. MacArthur Foundation, foundations need to enhance their support of public interest advocacy. "A critical role for philanthropy is the support of organizations monitoring and seeking beneficial changes in government and industry."[4]

The recommendations below outline ways in which the philanthropic community can assist public interest legal centers.

• *Foundations should be open to funding advocacy programs, in addition to service organizations, within their specific area of interest.* Public interest advocacy provides a way for the underrepresented in society to participate in the decisionmaking processes of democracy. It is a tool for social change that enfranchises and empowers the have-nots and triggers public debate and resolution on many important issues. A critical role for philanthropy is the support of organizations which monitor and promote changes in government, industry, and other established institutions.

• *Foundations should provide more funds in the form of general support to centers with established records of high performance.* Many foundations are only willing to support special projects, as opposed to providing general support funds. This means that a center may have to spend a substantial portion of its time planning new projects that will attract funding but will not be so different from the rest of the work being done as to radically distort the center's program. Often what is most important is the total impact an organization has in the community. It must have the flexibility to address vital issues which without funding might have to be overlooked.

• *Foundations should make exceptions to their policy of providing short-term seed money.* Many foundations have informal policies of only providing start-up funds to initiate new projects. They eschew long-term projects, even though it is generally acknowledged by both funders and organizations that their issues require commitments beyond the usual two to three years. As a result, centers must scramble from one foundation to another. Furthermore, attempting to convince local foundations to support cutting-edge activities can be frustrating and ultimately unsuccessful, forcing effective programs to terminate. Foundations should consider making renewal grants for excellent performance and changing developments and needs.

• *Foundations should provide support not just for litigation but for activities involved in implementing favorable court decrees.* Many of the foundations which support litigation have a preference for funding cases that are, in the words of one foundation trustee, "short and to the point." Overseeing the compliance phase is often costly, protracted, and labor-intensive. But it is nonetheless critical, ensuring that the goals of the litigation are realized and advanced by all parties.

• *Foundations should earmark funds for local community groups to hire public interest lawyers in private practice.* One way of protecting civil rights and the environment is to provide resources to community groups that seek social change. The groups can use these funds to retain private public interest practitioners. Alternatively, they can pay costs and expenses (payment of fees is prohibited by the IRS) to a public interest law center.

- *Both national and community foundations should support regional and local public interest law activities.* Foundations have a distinct preference for national issues and for programs addressing a national constituency. This preference has made it difficult for locally oriented centers to become established and grow. However, in this era of federal decentralization, it is even more important that grass roots groups have the resources to participate in public policy decisions.
- *Foundations should understand the value of, and work to preserve, diversity and specialization among different organizations in similar fields of public interest law.* The world of public interest law is not monolithic. The existence of several groups operating in the same field is a healthy phenomenon—it ensures that a variety of organizations with differing perspectives and strategies will address complex issues in a comprehensive way. The larger the number of leaders and citizens groups focusing on an issue, the greater its visibility and importance in the public policy arena.
- *Foundations should support public interest law activities through program-related investments as well as through grants.* Under the category of "program-related investments," as defined by the Internal Revenue Code, foundations can invest in buildings to house public interest organizations, which could share a library and other facilities. Additional space in such buildings could be rented out for the benefit of those centers. Foundations should also consider establishing "permanent development funds" by providing large amounts of support to groups with proven track records to give them stability.
- *Foundations should establish an institute for senior public interest lawyers which focuses on future goals and strategies.* Such an institute would provide lawyers the opportunity to concentrate on the implementation of long-term policies to bring about social and economic justice. It would relieve leaders in the field of their day-to-day responsibilities, allowing them to focus on broader goals and strategies. It could also help to train attorneys entering the field.

WHAT GOVERNMENT CAN DO

Public interest law has an important societal role and is at heart an ally of public institutions in governing fairly and well. Federal support for public interest law, particularly legal services for the poor, has diminished over the past several years. Programs have not been adequately funded, and the Legal Services Corporation's special support centers, which have played a significant role in law reform, have experienced cutbacks as well. In addition to these financial restraints, burdensome paperwork and frequent monitoring visits by Legal Services officials have had a debilitating effect on morale and performance.

The trend has been toward greater constraint on federal and state spending. However, given the current demand for free or inexpensive legal services, it is imperative that governmental units place a priority on funding legal representation. There is also a need for more generous funding of programs which assist such specific groups as the elderly, juveniles, and the mentally impaired.

Finally, both the Senate and the administration must take action to reverse the practice implemented by the Reagan administration to select judges based solely on their ideology rather than on their merits. President Reagan's legacy may well be best reflected in the number of conservative judges he has placed in the federal courts who lack a commitment to equal justice. In fact, during his second term, federal judgeships, and particularly Robert Bork's nomination, sparked the most intense debate of any issue in the administration's social policy agenda. Consequently, the citizenry feels more strongly about how a judge is selected and how the process is working.

The federal government can adopt many policies to help public interest law work better. Although the present conservative philosophy of the government and Congress may make it difficult to implement such policies, it is nevertheless important to suggest new programs to be implemented when the political climate changes.

- *Government should reassume its responsibilities to all its citizens.*
  The Reagan Administration has undermined two decades of political struggle to shape a government more responsive to the rights and needs of the vast majority of citizens. Instead of deliberately closing off citizen access to regulatory decisionmaking, government should institute regulatory reforms to encourage direct participation and to make agencies accountable to citizens. To increase public participation, government should be willing to finance citizen intervention in all regulatory decisions. Administrative agencies should resume activities designed to advance the public interest.
- *Congress should establish a commission to develop a plan for meeting the legal needs of the poor in the 1990s.* Recent surveys indicate that millions of people with legal problems go unrepresented each year because they cannot afford an attorney.[5] A commission of legal services lawyers, foundation executives, and bar leaders should develop a comprehensive picture of the legal needs of the poor and develop a strategy for use by the Legal Services Corporation,

paralegals, the American Bar Association and other bar groups, private firms, and consumer groups in meeting these needs.

- *Congress should substantially enlarge the Legal Services Corporation's budget.* There is an increasingly acute shortage of lawyers willing to represent the poor. According to the Project Advisory Group, which monitors the Corporation, the program nationwide should be funded at $400 million in fiscal year 1989. (This figure is exceedingly modest, but is regarded by advocates for the Corporation as politically feasible, given current fiscal restraints.) This amount would be used to hire more lawyers and increase funding for special support centers. Additional funding should also be used to reestablish the Corporation's Reginald Heber Smith program, which was instrumental in the past in recruiting minority lawyers to legal services and which was discontinued by the Reagan Administration.

- *The government should take strong action to address the underrepresentation of minorities and women on the federal bench and to base judicial selection on merit rather than ideology.* When President Jimmy Carter took office, he signed an Executive Order emphasizing that judicial selection would be based on merit selection and affirmative action. He created nominating commissions for circuit courts and issued guidelines for Senators to utilize in recommending judicial candidates. These processes, coupled with encouraging wide public participation in the process, provide a useful guidepost in the selection of nominees to the federal bench. Criteria for choosing judges should include open-mindedness, fairness, and commitment to equal justice.

- *The federal government should conduct the Combined Federal Campaign so that a wide range of organizations, including advocacy groups, are eligible to participate on the same basis as such groups as United Way of America and International Service Agencies.* The Combined Federal Campaign (CFC) was created in 1961 as a means for voluntary health and welfare agencies to solicit funds from federal employees. Since 1983, the administration has sought to bar advocacy groups from participating. In December 1987, Congress enacted a bill allowing federal employees to contribute to the charity of their choice, thereby guaranteeing eligibility for hundreds of charities. However, the Office of Personnel Management has been reluctant to implement the legislation and refuses to issue the regulations that carry out the Act's mandate.

- *The Internal Revenue Service should remove its prohibition on acceptance of client-paid fees by tax-exempt public interest law centers.* A public interest law firm should be permitted to accept fees from its clients as long as the group's educational and charitable purposes are adhered to, as long as the fees do not exceed the cost of providing the service, and as long as they do not inure to the benefit of individual attorneys. This would assist client groups to use the services of public interest law centers and pay, as they are able, for the services they receive. Churches, colleges, museums, theaters, and hospitals are exempt under Section 501(c)(3), even though they provide services in exchange for or in expectation of fees. The IRS should eliminate unnecessary distinction between public interest law firms and other charitable entities.

- *The federal government should commission a study highlighting successful federal and state financed programs which support public interest law.* There are numerous examples of state and local government programs designed to represent citizen groups. For example, the New Jersey Department of the Public Advocate, the largest state public counsel's office in the country, has been litigating public interest cases for more than ten years. Other states such as New York, Pennsylvania, and Wisconsin have specialized programs that concentrate on utility and insurance rates. These examples should be catalogued and studied so that other states may replicate them.

Attorneys' Fees

The recent congressional enactment of over a hundred fee-shifting statutes has had an enormous impact on the enforcement of civil rights and environmental law. These statutes have made it possible for thousands of impecunious plaintiffs to find lawyers and have been instrumental in promoting an active public interest bar.

As important as these statutes are to the representation of the poor, lawyers who have prevailed in such cases often experience difficulty in receiving their fees. Attempts to collect them are marked by delays between the resolution of merits and payment of the fees, reduced hourly rates, the incurrence of substantial out-of-pocket expenses which clients cannot afford to pay, and defendants who vigorously oppose fee awards. The result is that public interest law is becoming riskier and more costly, and many lawyers, particularly those in private practice, are turning down these cases because they are not financially competitive with other types of litigation.

In addition, the Supreme Court has written a number of opinions which limit the availability of fees, and Senators Hatch and Thurmond have on several occasions introduced bills which would substantially restrict the scope of many fee statutes. While the legislation has never passed, such debate has not fostered an atmosphere conducive to a discussion of positive reform. These factors have combined to render the availability of fees increasingly precarious.

The need for adequate counsel fees to attract competent attorneys willing to bring civil rights litigation is greater today than in the 1970s, when Congress enacted the bulk of the fees acts. Federal funds dedicated to enforcement of civil rights and public interest laws are increasingly limited, and the government generally sides with defendants in these cases. Below are recommendations which would facilitate the collection of fees and thus attract more lawyers to public interest case work.

- *Congress should reaffirm its support for the proposition that fees in civil rights cases be comparable to fees in other federal cases.* The legislative history of the Civil Rights Attorneys' Fees Awards Act of 1976 unequivocally states that it "is intended that the amount of fees awarded under [the Fees Act] be governed by the same standards which prevail in other types of equally complex Federal litigation, such as antitrust cases, and not be reduced because the rights involved be nonpecuniary in nature." Yet every commentator and court has noted the sizable disparity in both the standards applied and the fees awarded. Through legislation, Congress should reiterate its intention that courts determine reasonable rates in civil rights and other public interest litigation by applying the prevailing rates for other types of complex cases.
- *Congress should enact legislation overturning two harmful Supreme Court decisions, Evans v. Jeff D. and Marek v. Chesny.* A number of procedural problems have arisen concerning settlements. The Supreme Court recently wrote two opinions which will have immensely negative consequences for public interest lawyers. *Evans v. Jeff D.,* 1986, addresses the question of simultaneous negotiation of merits and fees. The Court allowed defense lawyers to offer lump sum monetary settlements covering plaintiffs' claims as well as fees. Such offers often place plaintiffs' lawyers in conflict with their clients. The other opinion, *Marek v. Chesny,* 1985, held that if a plaintiff rejects a settlement offer from the defendant and subsequently fails to obtain a judgment "more favorable" than the offer, the plaintiff forfeits all attorneys' fees incurred after the rejection of the offer. Both cases will substantially limit a plaintiff's ability to obtain fees.
- *The IRS requirement that centers not fund more than 50 percent of the total cost of their legal functions with fee awards should be waived for centers that are well established and fulfill a charitable role.* The current limitation is designed to prevent public interest

law firms from exploiting their tax exemption by generating fees
from cases inappropriate to the traditional rendering of legal services. For organizations that are established, proven, and controlled,
there is little if any risk of abuse, and the guideline should be
waived.

WHAT THE PRIVATE BAR CAN DO

Over the years, public interest law has gradually won the support
of the organized bar. Members of prominent firms sit on centers' boards
and litigation committees, handle cases, and provide financial support.
They serve as an important resource for representing those interests
that cannot obtain full representation in the marketplace. At the same
time, however, the expectation of strong involvement by major law
firms has not been realized. The bar serves only a small portion of
the legal needs of the poor, minorities, and citizens' groups. This record
must be improved. As one bar association official commented, "We
hold a monopoly on the provision of legal services, and persons who
hold such a monopoly have an obligation to help those who need to
navigate through the waters of the law."[6] *Pro bono* work can also benefit
the participating lawyers, their firms, and the community. It gives
private lawyers the opportunity to learn courtroom skills and, in some
instances, to work with public interest lawyers who are authorities in
their fields. The change of pace and different problems presented can
be stimulating.

Justice Brennan warns that when private practitioners "become increasingly removed from the social and public problems and concerns
that society deems more exigent and vital, they may become more
narrow in point of view, unduly circumscribed by the private and
parochial interests of their clients, lacking in perspective and vision."[7]
The Alliance for Justice recommends that the private bar strengthen
its commitment to public interest law in the following ways:

• *The American Bar Association should issue a report highlighting
  successful private firm* pro bono *programs.* Survival of public interest
  law is a matter of importance to the private bar, and there are
  several ways firms can foster this kind of work. First, they should
  take on more *pro bono* cases. Second, they should consider the
  model offered by New York Lawyers for the Public Interest (NYLPI),
  which is partially funded by New York City law firms and which,
  among other things, maintains a clearinghouse to match large
  public interest cases to firms who do *pro bono* work. Firms should
  also be encouraged to lend attorneys and paralegals for significant

periods of time (four to six months at a minimum) to public interest law offices.

- *State and local bars should establish programs to provide public interest legal services.* Organized by the New York City Bar Association, a group of the city's largest firms and corporate legal departments contributes thirty hours a year per lawyer to public service work. Another organization, the Los Angeles Public Counsel, which is the first bar-sponsored public interest office in the country, assists volunteer attorneys in providing legal assistance to the poor. Bar associations should also help to finance lawyers to act as house counsel to neighborhood citizens' groups.

- *Law firms should establish workplace solicitation programs to benefit public interest law centers.* Firms can provide substantial financial support by setting up workplace funding programs, similar to the United Way campaign, which would solicit contributions for public interest groups. The plan would allow lawyers to deduct money from their paychecks to be forwarded to organizations in the firm's city. The Alliance for Justice is spearheading an effort to persuade Washington, D.C. firms to conduct pledge campaigns for the Alliance's members. Payroll deduction is convenient for the lawyers and easy to administer.

- *More lawyers should participate in IOLTA programs.* Through IOLTAs, or Interest on Lawyers' Trust Accounts, lawyers pool money received in advance from clients. Separately, these amounts are generally too small to earn interest, but when combined in a single account they can generate sizable sums. The interest is sent to a special state fund and the bulk is distributed to legal services. There are currently forty-two programs across the country, and total income has topped $62 million. All IOLTA programs have restrictions on how funds may be used. Lawyers should advocate strongly that these funds be used not only for legal services offices but to support projects working for social and economic justice. North Carolina, Minnesota, New York, and Florida allocate a portion of these funds to support public interest legal representation.

WHAT LAW SCHOOLS CAN DO

Law schools have the responsibility of educating future generations of public interest lawyers. Today, however, socially minded law students face a dilemma: how to afford to go into public interest law when spiraling tuition and hefty loan burdens make it difficult to survive on the low salaries. The result of this dilemma is that many talented students are turning away from the field.

To combat this trend, law schools need to do a better job of instilling students with the skills and desire to be public interest lawyers. Legal educators throughout the country should increase student awareness of and involvement in the field through both course work and internships. They should also make students aware of the nature and history of public interest law. In addition, the Alliance for Justice recommends that law schools take the following steps to strengthen their commitment to public interest law:

- *Law schools should establish scholarships and loan programs to encourage students to take public service jobs.* Suggested approaches are to defer student loan repayment schedules, heavily discount loans, or forgive them altogether for students who take public service jobs for a set number of years. This last method was recently adopted by Harvard and Yale law schools. According to Harvard's Vice Dean Davis Smith, such programs make public interest "part of people's agenda after law school." Schools should also encourage alumni to endow public interest scholarships. At Stanford Law School, an alumna endowed a program which provides up to $3,500 to each of twenty students to work during the summer in government agencies and public interest law firms.
- *Law schools should make public interest law part of the legal education curriculum.* Clinical law programs expose students to new perspectives on legal problems and the ethical responsibilities of lawyers, as well as teaching them a range of practical skills. Clinics also benefit the community, contributing to the amount and variety of public interest representation available, and strengthen ties between the community and the law school. The Institute for Public Representation (IPR) at Georgetown University Law Center maintains a clinical program through which fifteen students each semester work on public interest litigation. City University of New York (CUNY) Law School at Queens College equips law students to undertake careers in government agencies and public interest law firms by providing a legal curriculum that focuses on public service. IPR and CUNY should both serve as models for other law schools.
- *Law schools should continue to promote the development of student-funded fellowship programs to sponsor public interest jobs for the summer.* At thirty-five schools across the country, students and alumni have responded to growing concern over the paucity of graduates entering the public interest field by donating a portion

of their summer or annual earnings to provide fellowships for public service jobs. Law schools which sponsor such programs include Berkeley, University of Michigan, Georgetown, University of Chicago, and Harvard. In 1985, these programs together raised a half million dollars.

- *Law schools should make public interest job opportunities a major focus of their placement activities.* Students need information about possibilities for using their legal education in the public interest arena. Placement offices should provide directories of public interest jobs and make every effort to link interested students with potential employers. The *Public Interest Career Guide* published by Tulane Law School's Office of Career Services offers the most comprehensive guide of any law school. Its format and information can easily be adapted by other schools to suit the needs of their own students.

WHAT PUBLIC INTEREST LAW CENTERS CAN DO

There is much that public interest legal groups themselves can do to work more effectively. They need to explore additional reforms and institutional innovations to further the goal of full and effective citizen participation in government. Creative ways to expand the provision of legal services need to be developed. One model is the program founded by Edgar Cahn, former dean of Antioch Law School, and recently adopted by the Florida legislature, which allows senior citizens to work for service credits for lawyers' time, rather than for money.

Ultimately, the success of consumer, environmental, and civil rights legal struggles depends on a more enduring institutional response. New strategies and techniques are needed to expand the donor base and build a politically committed citizenry. The following recommendations offer ways to facilitate this process.

- *In appropriate cases, public interest lawyers should seek relief in the form of trust funds to endow public interest advocacy.* This model is particularly well-suited to consumer class actions involving many class members with nominal individual damages. Indeed, the California Supreme Court recently endorsed the notion of a trust fund in *California v. Levi Strauss & Co.*. In this case, Levi Strauss was required to pay $12.5 million in refunds, but much of the money went unclaimed. Consumer advocates have proposed using it to establish a fund to promote consumer education and protection. Another example is the California Environmental Trust, established in 1985 to administer funds resulting from the settling of environmental lawsuits.

- *Public interest legal organizations should continue to strengthen ties with citizens' groups.* Input from these groups is essential if public interest lawyers are to effect needed social change. Exchange of information, technical asssistance, and coalition work are critically important and beneficial to both lawyers and local organizations. Lawyers should place more value on organizing and mobilizing citizen involvement in the governmental process.
- *Public interest law centers should unite to form alternative funds in order to raise money in the workplace.* Alternative funds—federations of charities, independent of United Way, that raise funds in the workplace—are becoming more common in cities across the country. These funds are appealing because they offer a lucrative, long-term source of income. One rapidly growing branch of the movement encompasses the women's funds, which raised $4.8 million in 1985 to benefit programs serving women. They are viable alternatives to the United Way for employees supporting the goals of the public interest law movement.
- *Centers should explore new ways to encourage citizen support of public interest advocacy.* The consumer check-off is one method of forming citizen-based organizations focused on particular issues, such as utility prices. For instance, consumers in Wisconsin may indicate on their bills their desire to join a utility accountability group which advocates for fair rates before courts, state legislators, and agencies.
- *Mass media's potential should be explored by public interest groups.* Media is the key to informing and influencing public opinion and mobilizing citizens to take action. Public interest lawyers should be willing to expend resources on integrating communication into each phase of their organizing process. Foundations should also consider funding a public relations component for groups.
- *Public interest organizations should continue to explore alternative means of obtaining redress and resolving disputes for their clients.* Programs that provide mediation and arbitration of disputes, lay advocates, and government bureaus that can handle citizen complaints are valuable and should be expanded. Within the context of litigation, such strategies as negotiation and mediation can often facilitate a quick resolution of the issues.

The Alliance will devote its energies over the next few years to implementing these recommendations. Steps have already been taken to carry out some of the proposals, and the Alliance and its members will work with civic groups, government officials, Congress, and the philanthropic community to achieve the other goals. The Alliance will also continue to consider additional recommendations and incorporate them in its future agenda.

The time is ripe for a new administration to review and reflect upon the recommendations. Adequate and affordable legal services have yet to become a reality for many of our citizens. Too many Americans lack the kind of expertise that is needed to cope with an increasingly complex system of government entitlements and regulations. Some of these problems can be remedied by public interest law, an approach which offers citizens the means to participate in a democracy. Advancing and expanding public interest law will mean that all sides to an issue will be heard from and considered in the important policy debates facing us in the future.

Notes

1. "Looking Ahead: The Future of Public Interest Law." Address by Ralph Nader to the Alliance for Justice conference, "Preserving Access to Justice," June 11, 1985.

2. Alliance for Justice interview with Anh Tu, Project Advisory Group, March 14, 1987.

3. *Emergency Needs Project. Report and Recommendations.* Convenor: The Minneapolis Foundation. November 21, 1983.

4. Alliance for Justice interview with Elizabeth McCormack, Vice-President of the J.D.R. 3rd Fund and Director of the John D. and Catherine T. MacArthur Foundation, May 6, 1987.

5. Alliance for Justice interview with Alan Houseman, Executive Director, Center for Law and Social Policy, March 15, 1987.

6. David Margolick, "Big Law Firms Stepping Up Volunteer Services in the City," *New York Times* (May 2, 1984), pp. A1, D25.

7. Justice William J. Brennan, "The Responsibilities of the Legal Profession," 54 *ABA Journal* (Feb. 1968), pp. 123–24.

Appendix A

DIRECTORY OF PUBLIC INTEREST
LAW CENTERS

ADVOCACY CENTER FOR THE ELDERLY AND DISABLED, 1001 Howard Avenue, Suite 300A, New Orleans, LA 70013. 504/522-2337. (Formerly Louisiana Center for the Public Interest; Advocates for the Developmentally Disabled.)

Branches: Alexandria and Shreveport, LA.

ADVOCACY, INC., 7800 Shoal Creek Boulevard, Suite 171E, Austin, TX 78757. 512/454-4816.

ADVOCATES FOR BASIC LEGAL EQUALITY, INC., 740 Spitzer Building, Toledo, OH 43604. 419/255-0814.

Branches: Findlay, Fremont and Defiance, OH.

ADVOCATES FOR CHILDREN OF NEW YORK, 24–16 Bridge Plaza South, Long Island City, NY 11101. 718/729-8866.

ALASKA YOUTH AND PARENT FOUNDATION, 3745 Community Park Loop, Suite 202, Anchorage, AK 99508. 907/274-6541.

ALIEN RIGHTS PROJECT, Lawyers' Committee for Civil Rights Under Law, 1400 I Street, NW, Suite 400, Washington, DC 20005. 202/682-5900.

AMERICAN ASSOCIATION FOR PERSONAL PRIVACY, 1782 Pacific Avenue, San Francisco, CA 94109. 415/474-8408. (Formerly the National Committee for Sexual Civil Liberties.)

Branch: Princeton, NJ.

AMERICAN CIVIL LIBERTIES UNION/ACLU FOUNDATION, 132 West 43rd Street, New York, NY 10017. 212/944-9800.

Regional offices: Denver, CO; Atlanta, GA. Fifty state and local affiliates throughout the country.

ACLU NATIONAL SECURITY LITIGATION PROJECT, 122 Maryland Avenue, NE, Washington, DC 20002. 202/544-1681.

AMERICAN COUNCIL OF THE BLIND, 1211 Connecticut Avenue, NW, Suite 506, Washington, DC 20036. 202/833-1251.

APPALACHIAN RESEARCH AND DEFENSE FUND, 1116-B Kanawha Blvd. East, Charleston, WV 25301. 304/344-9687.

Branches: Beckley, Fayetteville, Hamline, Logan, Pineville, Princeton, Welch and Williamson, WV.

ARKANSAS ADVOCATES FOR CHILDREN AND FAMILIES, 931 Donaghey Building, Little Rock, AR 72201.

ARKANSAS JUVENILE JUSTICE INSTITUTE, 118 National Old Line Building, Little Rock, AR 72201.

ARIZONA CENTER FOR LAW IN THE PUBLIC INTEREST, 112 North Central, Suite 400, Phoenix, AZ 85004. 602/252-4904.
Branch: Tuscon, AZ.

ASIAN-AMERICAN LEGAL DEFENSE AND EDUCATION FUND. 99 Hudson Street, 12th Floor, New York, NY 10013. 212/966-5932.

ASIAN LAW CAUCUS, 1322 Webster, Suite 210, Oakland, CA 94612. 415/835-1474.
Branch: San Francisco, CA.

ASSOCIATION OF CHILD ADVOCATES, 3615 Superior Avenue, Bldg. 31, Suite 2B, Cleveland, OH 44114. 216/881-2225.

AVIATION CONSUMER ACTION PROJECT, PO Box 19029, 1346 Connecticut Avenue, NW, Suite 717, Washington, DC 20036. 202/223-4498.

BAY AREA CENTER FOR LAW AND THE DEAF, 125 Parrott, San Leandro, CA 94577. 415/895-1610.

BUSINESS AND PROFESSIONAL PEOPLE FOR THE PUBLIC INTEREST (BPI), 109 North Dearborn Street, Suite 1300, Chicago, IL 60602. 312/641-5570.

CALIFORNIA RURAL LEGAL ASSISTANCE, 2111 Mission Street, Suite 401, San Francisco, CA 94110. 415/864-3405.
Branches: 14 branch offices across the state.

CAPITAL LEGAL FOUNDATION, 700 E Street, SE, Washington, DC 20003. 202/546-5533.

CAROLINA LEGAL ASSISTANCE, Mental Disability Law Project, Box 2446, Raleigh, NC 27602. 919/834-0723.

CENTER FOR APPLIED LEGAL STUDIES, Georgetown University Law Center, 600 New Jersey Avenue, NW, Washington, DC 20001. 202/662-9099.

CENTER FOR AUTO SAFETY, 2001 S Street, NW, Suite 328, Washington, DC 20009. 202/828-7700.

CENTER FOR CONSTITUTIONAL RIGHTS, 853 Broadway, 14th Floor, New York, NY 10003. 212/674-3303.
Branch: Greenville, MS.

CENTER FOR LAW AND EDUCATION, Six Appian Way, 3rd Floor, Cambridge, MA 02138. 617/495-4666.

CENTER FOR LAW AND HEALTH SCIENCE, c/o Prof. H. Beyer, Boston University Law School, 765 Commonwealth Avenue, Boston, MA 02215. 617/353-2904.

CENTER FOR LAW AND SOCIAL POLICY, 1616 P Street, NW, 3rd Floor, Washington, DC 20036. 202/328-5140.

CENTER FOR LAW IN THE PUBLIC INTEREST, 10951 W. Pico Blvd., Los Angeles, CA 90064. 213/470-3000.

CENTER FOR PUBLIC REPRESENTATION, 520 University Avenue, Madison, WI 53703. 608/251-4008.

CENTER FOR RURAL AFFAIRS, P.O. Box 405, Walthill, NE 68067. 402/846-5428. (Formerly Small Farm Advocacy Project.)
Branch: Hartington, NE.
CENTER FOR SCIENCE IN THE PUBLIC INTEREST, 1501 16th Street, NW, Washington, DC 20036. 202/332-9110.
CENTER ON SOCIAL WELFARE POLICY AND LAW, 95 Madison Avenue, Room 701, New York, NY 10016. 212/679-3709.
Branch: Washington, DC.
CHICAGO LAWYERS' COMMITTEE FOR CIVIL RIGHTS UNDER LAW, INC., 220 South State Street, Suite 300, Chicago, IL 60604. 312/939-5797.
CHICANO EDUCATION PROJECT, 1410 Grant Street, Suite B104, Denver, CO 80204. 303/830-1052.
Branches: Arkansas Valley and Rocky Ford, AR; Ignacio and San Luis Valley Center, CO.
CHILD ADVOCACY CENTER, Park Lane Bldg., Suite 1113, 225 I Street, NW, Washington, DC 20006.
CHILD ADVOCACY, INC., Park View Building, Suite 306, 1879 N. University Drive, Ft. Lauderdale, FL 33322.
CHILD ADVOCACY PROJECT, 88 Walton Street, NW, Atlanta, GA 30303.
CHILDREN'S DEFENSE FUND, 122 C Street, NW, Washington, DC 20001. 202/628-8787.
Branches: Jackson, MS; Columbus, OH.
CHILDREN'S RIGHTS GROUP, 693 Mission Street, Suite 600, San Francisco, CA 94105. 415/495-7283.
Branches: Los Angeles and Santa Rosa, CA; Denver, CO; Helena, MT; Pierre, SD.
CHILDREN'S RIGHTS PROJECT of the ACLU, 132 West 43rd Street, New York, NY 10017. 212/944-9800.
COLORADO COALITION OF LEGAL SERVICES PROGRAMS, 770 Grant Street, Suite 206, Denver, CO 80203. 303/830-1551.
COLORADO LAWYERS' COMMITTEE, 1441 18th Street, Suite 50, Denver, CO 80202. 303/297-3115.
COMMUNICATIONS MEDIA CENTER, New York Law School, 57 Worth Street, New York, NY 10013. 212/966-2053.
COMMUNITY DEVELOPMENT LEGAL ASSISTANCE CENTER, 99 Hudson Street, New York, NY 10013. 212/219-1800.
COMMUNITY HEALTH LAW PROJECT, 55 Washington Street, East Orange, NJ 07017. 201/672-6050.
Branches: Camden, Elizabeth and Trenton, NJ.
CONNECTICUT FUND FOR THE ENVIRONMENT, 152 Temple Street, Suite 412, New Haven, CT 06510. 203/787-0646.
CONNECTICUT WOMEN'S EDUCATIONAL AND LEGAL FUND, INC., 22 Maple Avenue, Hartford, CT 06114. 203/247-6090.
CONSERVATION LAW FOUNDATION OF NEW ENGLAND, INC., Three Joy Street, Boston, MA 02108. 617/742-2540.
CONSTITUTIONAL LITIGATION CLINIC, Rutgers University Law School, 15 Washington Street, Newark, NJ 07102. 201/648-5687.

CONSUMERS UNION, Litigation office, 2001 S Street, NW, Washington, DC 20009. 202/462-6262.

Branches: San Francisco, CA; Mount Vernon, NY; Austin, TX.

DISABILITY RIGHTS CENTER, 2500 Q Street, NW, Washington, DC 20007. 202/223-3304.

DISABILITY RIGHTS EDUCATION AND DEFENSE FUND, INC., 2032 San Pablo Avenue, Berkeley, CA 94702. 415/644-2555. TDD: 415/644-2629. Branch: Washington, DC.

EDUCATION LAW CENTER, INC., 225 S. 15th Street, Suite 2100, Philadelphia, PA 19102. 215/732-6655.

Branch: Newark, NJ.

EMPLOYMENT LAW CENTER of the Legal Aid Society of San Francisco, 1663 Mission Street, Suite 400, San Francisco, CA 94103. 415/864-8848.

ENVIRONMENTAL DEFENSE FUND, 444 Park Avenue South, New York, NY 10016. 212/686-4191.

Branches: Berkeley, CA; Boulder, CO; Washington, DC; Richmond, VA.

EQUAL RIGHTS ADVOCATES, 1370 Mission Street, 4th Floor, San Francisco, CA 94103. 415/621-0505.

FAMILY ADVOCACY COUNCIL, 15 Western Promenade, Auburn, ME 04210.

FLORIDA INSTITUTIONAL LEGAL SERVICES, 2614 South West 34th Street, Gainesville, FL 32608. 904/373-3179.

FLORIDA JUSTICE INSTITUTE, INC., 1401 AmeriFirst Bldg., 1 Southeast Third Avenue, Miami, FL 33131. 305/358-2081.

FOOD RESEARCH AND ACTION CENTER (FRAC), 1319 F Street, NW, Suite 500, Washington, DC 20004. 202/393-5060.

FREEDOM OF INFORMATION CLEARINGHOUSE, 2000 P Street, NW, Suite 700, Washington, DC 20036. 202/783-3704.

GAY AND LESBIAN ADVOCATES AND DEFENDERS/PARK SQUARE ADVOCATES, INC., 100 Boylston Street, Suite 900, Boston, MA 02116. 617/426-1350.

GOVERNMENT ACCOUNTABILITY PROJECT, 25 E Street, NW, Washington, DC 20001. 202/347-0460.

GULF AND GREAT PLAINS LEGAL FOUNDATION, 101 West 11th Street, Kansas City, MO 64105. 816/474-6600.

Branch: Houston, TX.

HARRISON INSTITUTE FOR PUBLIC LAW, Georgetown University Law Center, 25 E Streeet, NW, Washington, DC 20001. 202/662-9600.

HOUSING ADVOCATES, INC., 353 Leader Building, Cleveland, OH 44114. 216/579-0575.

ILLINOIS PRISONS AND JAIL, John Howard Association, 67 E. Madison Avenue, Chicago, IL 60603.

IMMIGRATION LAW CLINIC, Columbia University School of Law, 435 West 116th Street, New York, NY 10027. 212/280-4291.

INDIAN LAW RESOURCE CENTER, 601 E Street, SE, Washington, DC 20003. 202/547-2800.

INDUSTRIAL COOPERATIVE ASSOCIATION, Legislative Support Project, 249 Elm Street, Somerville, MA 02114. 617/628-7330.

Branch: Port Washington, NY.

INSTITUTE FOR CHILD ADVOCACY, 2800 Euclid Avenue, Suite 314, Cleveland, OH 44115. 216/579-1460.

INSTITUTE FOR PUBLIC REPRESENTATION, Georgetown University Law Center, 600 New Jersey Avenue, NW, Washington, DC 20001. 202/662-9535.

INTERNATIONAL HUMAN RIGHTS LAW GROUP, 733 15th Street, NW, Suite 1000, Washington, DC 20005. 202/639-8016.

JUVENILE JUSTICE LAW CLINIC, Georgetown University Law Center, 25 E Street, NW, Washington, DC 20001. 202/662-9590.

JUVENILE LAW CENTER OF PHILADELPHIA, 112 South 16th Street, 7th Floor, Philadelphia, PA 19102. 215/625-0551.

KENTUCKY YOUTH ADVOCATES, 2024 Woodford Place, Louisville, KY 40205.

LAMBDA LEGAL DEFENSE AND EDUCATION FUND, 666 Broadway, New York, NY 10012. 212/995-8585.

LAWYERS COMMITTEE FOR CIVIL RIGHTS UNDER LAW (LCCRUL), National Office, 1400 I Street, NW, Suite 400, Washington, DC 20005. 202/371-1212.

Branch: Jackson, MS.

Affiliated offices: Los Angeles and San Francisco, CA; Denver, CO; Washington, DC; Atlanta, GA; Chicago, IL; Boston, MA; Philadelphia, PA (Los Angeles—Public Counsel; Denver—Colorado Lawyers' Committee; Boston—LCCRUL of the Boston Bar; Philadelphia—Public Interest Law Center of Philadelphia).

LEAGUE OF WOMEN VOTERS EDUCATION FUND, Litigation Department, 1730 M Street, NW, Washington, DC 20036. 202/429-1965.

LEGAL ACTION CENTER. 19 West 44th Street, New York, NY 10036. 212/997-0110.

LEGAL COUNSEL FOR THE ELDERLY, 1331 H Street, NW, Washington, DC 20005. 202/234-0970.

Branch: Washington, DC.

LEGAL ENVIRONMENTAL ASSISTANCE FOUNDATION, 203 N. Gadsden Street, Tallahassee, FL 32301. 904/681-2591.

Branches: Birmingham, AL; Atlanta, GA; Knoxville, TN.

LEGAL SERVICES FOR CHILDREN, INC., 149 9th Street, Top Floor, San Francisco, CA 94103. 415/863-3762.

LEGAL SERVICES FOR THE ELDERLY, 132 West 43rd Street, New York, NY 10036. 212/391-0120.

LESBIAN RIGHTS PROJECT, 1370 Mission Street, 4th Floor, San Francisco, CA 94103. 415/621-0674.

MASSACHUSETTS CORRECTIONAL LEGAL SERVICES, INC., 8 Winter Street, 9th Floor, Boston, MA 02108. 617/482-2773.

MASSACHUSETTS LAW REFORM INSTITUTE, 69 Canal Street, Boston, MA 02114. 617/742-9250.

MISSISSIPPI PRISONERS' DEFENSE, 233 N. Farish Street, Jackson, MS 39201.

MASS PIRG (Public Interest Research Group), 37 Temple Place, Boston, MA 02111. 617/423-1796.
Branches: Amherst, Worcester and New Bedford, MA. (Also at 19 college campuses around the state.)

MEDIA ACCESS PROJECT, 1609 Connecticut Avenue, NW, Washington, DC 20009. 202/232-4300.

MENTAL HEALTH ADVOCACY PROJECT, 711 East San Fernando, San Jose, CA 95112. 408/294-9730.

MENTAL HEALTH LAW PROJECT, 2020 L Street, NW, Suite 800, Washington, DC 20036. 202/467-5730.

MEXICAN AMERICAN LEGAL DEFENSE AND EDUCATION FUND, 28 Geary Street, 6th Floor, San Francisco, CA 94108. 415/981-5800.
Branches: Los Angeles, CA; Denver, CO; Washington, DC; Chicago, IL; San Antonio, TX.

MICHIGAN LEGAL SERVICES, 900 Michigan Building, 220 Bagley, Detroit, MI 48226. 313/964-4130.
Branch: Lansing, MI.

MID-ATLANTIC LEGAL FOUNDATION, 400 Market Street, 3rd Floor, Philadelphia, PA 19106. 215/238-1367.
Branch: New York, NY.

MIGRANT LEGAL ACTION PROGRAM, 2001 S Street, NW, Washington, DC 20009. 202/462-7744.

MOUNTAIN STATES LEGAL FOUNDATION, 1200 Lincoln Street, Suite 600, Denver, CO 80203. 303/861-0244.

NAACP LEGAL DEFENSE AND EDUCATION FUND, 99 Hudson Street, 16th Floor, New York, NY 10013. 212/219-1900.
Branch: Washington, DC.

NATIONAL ASSOCIATION OF THE DEAF LEGAL DEFENSE FUND, 800 Florida Avenue, NE, P.O. Box 2304, Washington, DC 20002. 202/651-5461.

NATIONAL AUDUBON SOCIETY, 645 Pennsylvania Avenue, SE, Washington, DC 20003. 202/547-9009.

NATIONAL CENTER FOR IMMIGRANTS' RIGHTS, 256 S. Occidental Blvd., Los Angeles, CA 90057. 213/388-8693.

NATIONAL CENTER FOR LAW AND THE DEAF, 800 Florida Avenue, NE, Washington, DC 20002. 202/651-5454. TTY: 202/651-5457.

NATIONAL CENTER ON WOMEN AND FAMILY LAW, 799 Broadway, Room 402, New York, NY 10003. 212/674-8200.

NATIONAL CENTER FOR YOUTH LAW, 1663 Mission Street, 5th Floor, San Francisco, CA 94103. 415/543-3307.

NATIONAL COALITION FOR THE HOMELESS, 105 East 22nd Street, New York, NY 10010. 212/460-8110.

NATIONAL CONSUMER LAW CENTER, 11 Beacon Street, Room 821, Boston, MA 02108. 617/523-8010.
Branch: Washington, DC.

NATIONAL ECONOMIC DEVELOPMENT AND LAW CENTER, 1950 Addison Street, Suite 200, Berkeley, CA 94704. 415/548-2600.
Branch: Washington, DC.
NATIONAL EMPLOYMENT LAW PROJECT, INC., 475 Riverside Drive, Suite 240, New York, NY 10115. 212/870-2121.
Branch: Washington, DC.
NATIONAL FEMALE ADVOCACY PROJECT, 376 South Stone, Tuscon, AZ 85701.
NATIONAL GAY RIGHTS ADVOCATES, 540 Castro Street, San Francisco, CA 94114. 415/863-3624.
NATIONAL HEALTH LAW PROGRAM, 2639 S. LaCienega Blvd., Los Angeles, CA 90034. 213/204-6010.
Branch: Washington, DC.
NATIONAL JUVENILE LAW CENTER, 3701 Lindell Blvd., P.O. Box 14200, St. Louis, MO 63178. 314/652-5555.
NATIONAL ORGANIZATION FOR THE REFORM OF MARIJUANA LAWS (NORML), 2001 S Street, NW, Suite 640, Washington, DC 20009. 202/483-5500.
Chapters in 40 states.
NATIONAL ORGANIZATION FOR WOMEN LEGAL DEFENSE AND EDUCATION FUND, 99 Hudson Street, New York, NY 10013. 212/925-6635.
Branch: Washington, DC.
NATIONAL PRISON PROJECT of the ACLU Foundation, 1616 P Street, NW, Washington, DC 20036. 202/331-0500.
NATIONAL SENIOR CITIZENS LAW CENTER, 2025 M Street, NW, Suite 400, Washington, DC 20036. 202/887-5280.
NATIONAL WILDLIFE FEDERATION, Resources' Defense Division, 1400 16th Street, NW, Washington, DC 20036. 202/797-6800.
Resource Centers: Anchorage, AK; Boulder, CO; Missoula, MT; Eugene, OR.
NATIONAL WOMEN'S LAW CENTER, 1616 P Street, NW, Suite 100, Washington, DC 20036. 202/328-5160.
NATIONAL WOMEN'S LAW FUND, 1101 Euclid Street, Suite 400, Cleveland, OH 44115. 216/621-3443.
NATIVE AMERICAN RIGHTS FUND, 1506 Broadway, Boulder, CO 80302. 303/447-8760.
Branch: Washington, DC.
NATURAL RESOURCES DEFENSE COUNCIL, 122 East 42nd Street, New York, NY 10017. 212/949-0049.
Affiliated offices: San Francisco, CA; Denver, CO; Washington, DC.
NEW ENGLAND LEGAL FOUNDATION, 55 Union Street, Boston, MA 02108. 617/367-0174.
NEW YORK LAWYERS FOR THE PUBLIC INTEREST, INC., 135 East 15th Street, New York, NY 10003. 212/777-7707.
NORTHWEST ENVIRONMENTAL DEFENSE CENTER, 10015 Southwest Terwilliger Blvd., Portland, OR 97219. 503/244-1181, ext. 707.

NORTHWEST LABOR AND EMPLOYMENT LAW OFFICE, 705 Second Avenue, Seattle, WA 98104. 206/623-1590.

NORTHWEST WOMEN'S LAW CENTER, 119 South Main Street, Suite 330, Seattle, WA 98104. 206/682-9552.

OFICINA LEGAL DEL PUEBLO UNIDO, P.O. Box 1493, San Juan, TX 78589. 512/787-8171.

1000 FRIENDS OF OREGON, 519 Southwest Third, Room 400, Portland, OR 97204. 503/223-4396.

PACIFIC LEGAL FOUNDATION, 455 Capitol Mall, Suite 465, Sacramento, CA 95814. 916/444-0154.
Branch: Washington, DC.

PACIFIC NORTHWEST RESOURCES CLINIC, University of Oregon School of Law, Eugene, OR 97403. 503/681-3823.

PRISON LAW CLINIC, Rutgers University School of Law, 15 Washington Street, Newark, NJ 07102. 201/648-5978.

PROJECT JUSTICE AND EQUALITY, 475 Broadway, Gary, IN 46402. 219/883-0384.
Branch: Valparaiso, IN.

PUBLIC ADVOCATES, INC., 1535 Mission Street, San Francisco, CA 94103. 415/431-7430.

PUBLIC CITIZEN LITIGATION GROUP, 2000 P Street, NW, Suite 700, Washington, DC 20036. 202/785-3704.

PUBLIC COUNSEL, 3535 West 6th Street, Suite 100, Los Angeles, CA 90020. 213/385-2977.

PUBLIC EDUCATION ASSOCIATION, Litigation Department, 20 West 40th Street, New York, NY 10018. 212/354-6100.

PUBLIC INTEREST LAW CENTER OF PHILADELPHIA, 1315 Walnut Street, Suite 1600, Philadelphia, PA 19107. 215/735-7200.

PUBLIC INTEREST LAW CLINIC, Practicing Law Center, American University School of Law, 4400 Massachusetts Avenue, NW, Washington, DC 20016. 202/686-2629. (Formerly associated with the National Veterans' Law Center; now see Vietnam Veterans of America Legal Services.)

PUBLIC ISSUE ADVOCATES, Capitol Hall, 6th Floor, 115 W. Allegan, Lansing, MI 48933. 517/372-1000.

PUERTO RICAN LEGAL DEFENSE AND EDUCATION FUND, INC., 99 Hudson Street, New York, NY 10013. 212/219-3360.

REPORTERS' COMMITTEE FOR FREEDOM OF THE PRESS, 800 18th Street, NW, Suite 300, Washington DC 20006. 202/466-6313.

REPRODUCTIVE FREEDOM PROJECT of the ACLU, 132 West 43rd Street, New York, NY 10017. 212/944-9800.

ROGER BALDWIN FOUNDATION of the ACLU, 220 S. State Street, Suite 816, Chicago, IL 60604. 312/427-7330.

SAN FRANCISCO LAWYERS' COMMITTEE FOR URBAN AFFAIRS, 625 Market Street, Suite 915, San Francisco, CA 94105. 415/543-9444.

SANTA CLARA COUNTY BAR ASSOCIATION LAW FOUNDATION, INC., 111 N. Market Street, Suite 712, San Jose, CA 95115. 408/294-9730. (Affiliated with the Mental Health Advocacy Project and Public Interest Law Firm, San Jose.)

SIERRA CLUB LEGAL DEFENSE FUND, 2044 Fillmore Street, San Francisco, CA 94115. 415/567-6100.
Branches: Juneau, AK; Denver, CO; Washington, DC.

SOUTHEASTERN LEGAL FOUNDATION, INC., 2900 Chamblee-Tucker Road, Building 4, Atlanta, GA 30341. 404/458-8313.

SOUTHERN ENVIRONMENTAL LAW CENTER, 201 West Main Street, Suite 14, Charlottesville, VA 22901. 804/977-4090.

SOUTHERN LEGAL COUNSEL, INC., 115 North East 7th Avenue, Suite A, Gainesville, FL 32601. 904/377-8288.

SOUTHERN POVERTY LAW CENTER, 1001 S. Hull Street, Montgomery, AL 36104. 205/264-0286.

SOUTHERN PRISONERS' DEFENSE COMMITTEE, 600 Healy Building, 57 Forsyth Street, Atlanta, GA 30303. 404/688-1202.

TRIAL LAWYERS FOR PUBLIC JUSTICE, P.C., 2000 P Street, NW, Washington, DC 20036. 202/463-8600.

TRUSTEES FOR ALASKA, INC., 833 Gambell Street, Suite B, Anchorage, AK 99501. 907/276-4244.

UCLA COMMUNICATIONS LAW PROGRAM, School of Law, University of California at Los Angeles, Los Angeles, CA 90024. 213/825-6211.

UNTAPPED RESOURCES, INC., 60 First Avenue, New York, NY 10009. 212/532-4422.

URBAN INDIAN LAW PROJECT, Phoenix Indian Center, 3302 North 7th Street, Phoenix, AZ 85014.

URBAN LEGAL CLINIC, Rutgers University School of Law, 15 Washington Street, Newark, NJ 07102. 201/648-5576.

VIETNAM VETERANS OF AMERICA LEGAL SERVICES, 2001 S Street, NW, Suite 702, Washington, DC 20009. 202/332-2700. (Formerly the National Veterans' Law Center.)

WASHINGTON LAWYERS' COMMITTEE FOR CIVIL RIGHTS UNDER LAW, 1400 I Street, NW, Suite 450, Washington, DC 20005. 202/371-1212.

WESTERN CENTER ON LAW AND POVERTY, INC., 3535 W. Sixth Street, Los Angeles, CA 90020. 213/487-7211.

WESTERN LAW CENTER FOR THE HANDICAPPED, Loyola School of Law, 1441 W. Olympic Blvd., P.O. Box 15019, Los Angeles, CA 90015. 213/736-1031.

WOMEN'S ADVOCACY PROJECT, 121 East 8th Street, Suite 412A, Austin, TX 78701. 512/477-8113.

WOMEN'S EQUITY ACTION LEAGUE (WEAL), 1250 I Street, NW, Suite 305, Washington, DC 20005. 202/898-1588.

WOMEN'S LAW PROJECT, 125 South 9th Street, Suite 401, Philadelphia, PA 19107. 215/928-9801.

WOMEN'S LEGAL DEFENSE FUND, 2000 P Street, NW, Suite 400, Washington, DC 20036. 202/887-0364.

WOMEN'S RIGHTS LITIGATION CLINIC, Rutgers University School of Law, 15 Washington Street, Newark, NJ 07102. 201/648-5637.

WOMEN'S RIGHTS PROJECT of the ACLU, 132 West 43rd Street, New York, NY 10036. 212/944-9800.
Branch: Richmond, VA.
YOUTH POLICY AND LAW CENTER, 30 W. Mifflin, Room 904, Madison, WI 53703. 608/263-5533.
Branch: Milwaukee, WI.

Appendix B

ALLIANCE FOR JUSTICE
NATIONAL SURVEY OF PUBLIC INTEREST LAW PROGRAMS

This survey is designed to provide basic information about existing public interest law programs, their activities, and sources of funding. The data we are collecting are confidential and will be reported in statistical aggregate form only; no institution or organization will be identified.

Please take a few minutes to complete this questionnaire as accurately as possible and return it in the enclosed envelope today. Please type or print.

Name of Organization: _____

Address: _____

Telephone Number: _____ Director's Name _____

BACKGROUND INFORMATION

1. What is your organization's IRS tax status?

    501(c)(3) public charity _____
    501(c)(4) _____
    Other (specify) _____

    If you are a 501(c)(3) public charity organization, have you elected to lobby under the provisions of the Tax Reform Act of 1976?

    Yes _____
    No _____

2. In what year was your organization established? _____

3. Does your organization have any branch offices?

    Yes _____
    No _____

    IF YES: Please enter the name of each city in which a branch is located below:

147

STAFF

4. (a) How many salaried attorneys does your organization currently employ? (Include positions now vacant.)

   _____

   (b) How many other salaried professionals (administrators, researchers, writers, lobbyists, etc.) does your organization employ? (Include positions now vacant.)

   _____

   (c) If your organization conducts a legal education clinic as part of its activities, what is the average number of students engaged in legal work (per academic year)?

   _____

5. Does your organization use outside attorneys, either paid or unpaid, to perform any of its legal work? (Include only program work).

   Yes _____
   No _____

   IF YES: Approximately what percentage of your organization's legal work is performed by outside attorneys you pay and/or by outside attorneys you do not pay?

   Outside attorneys you pay _____ %

   Outside attorneys you do not pay _____ %

6. Please break down the number of salaried lawyers in your organization according to their current annual earnings range.

   ANNUAL EARNINGS (In Thousands)

Number of Lawyers						
Under $15	$16-20	$21-30	$31-40	$41-50	$51-60	Over $60

7. Please break down the number of attorneys you employ according to the length of time they have been out of law school.

Number of Lawyers						
Total	Years 0-2	Years 3-5	Years 6-8	Years 9-11	Years 12-15	Years Over 15

ACTIVITIES

8. During the past year, approximately what percentage of your organization's total effort was devoted to the following activities:

Litigation _____%

Other legal work (Include negotiation, administrative agency rule-making, adjudication, monitoring, etc.) _____%

Legislative Work (include lobbying, testifying, research, drafting model legislation) _____%

Individual Legal Assistance (assistance on case-by-case basis or providing information in response to individual inquiries) _____%

Internal Administration (include fund-raising, In-house activities) _____%

Community Organizing/Public Education _____%

Other (please specify) _____%

TOTAL   100 %

9. During the past year, approximately what percentage of your organization's total effort was devoted to each of the following issue areas:

Environmental Protection _____%
Consumer Protection _____%
Employment _____%
Education _____%
Housing _____%
Health Care _____%
Welfare Benefits _____%
Nuclear _____%
International/Immigration _____%
Occupational Safety and Health _____%
Voting _____%
Civil Rights _____%
Civil Liberties _____%
Rural Development _____%
Communications/Media Reform _____%
Free Enterprise/Limiting Fed'l Gov't_____%
Other _____%

TOTAL   100 %

10. During the past year, approximately what percentage of your organization's total effort was designed to benefit each of the following target population or client groups:

General population	_____ %
Poor, in general	_____ %
Blacks	_____ %
Spanish-speaking people	_____ %
Native Americans (Indians)	_____ %
Other racial/ethnic minorities	_____ %
Women	_____ %
Children	_____ %
Elderly	_____ %
Mentally disabled	_____ %
Prisoners	_____ %
Physically disabled	_____ %
Homosexuals	_____ %
Immigrants	_____ %
Workers	_____ %
Veterans	_____ %
Other (specify) _____	_____ %

TOTAL   100 %

11. Estimate what percentage of your current law program is concerned with the actions of:

Federal Government Agencies	_____ %
Congress	_____ %
State Government Agencies	_____ %
State Legislatures	_____ %
Local Government Agencies	_____ %
Business Corporations	_____ %
Other (specify) _____	_____ %

_____

_____

TOTAL   100 %

12. If your center does a significant amount of work directly with state and local organizations, describe the number and type of organizations and nature of your activities with them.

FINANCIAL RESOURCES

13. What are the dates of your fiscal year? _____

14. Please indicate the amount of income, if any, your
     organization has received from each of the following
     sources in its most recent fiscal year (if fiscal year
     ends June 30, please estimate for this fiscal year).

     TOTAL INCOME   %_____

     Foundation grants   _____

     Membership dues   _____

     Contributions, gifts   _____

     Federal contracts, grants*   _____

     Sale of materials   _____

     Churches   _____

     Corporations   _____

     Established bar   _____

     State/local funds   _____

     Court-awarded or approved fees   _____

     Workplace fundraising campaigns
        (i.e. Combined Federal Campaign)   _____

     Lawyer trust fund accounts   _____

     Loans   _____

     Other (please specify) _____   _____

     _____

     *Include federal funds administered by non-federal
      agencies.

16. Please specify any substantial in-kind contributions (e.g.,
     donated office space, equipment or facilities) received by your
     organization in FY 1982-1983. Please indicate the nature of the
     contribution, its source and approximate value.

17. Please indicate names of your five top funders.

18. (a) Approximately what percentage of your cases are those where statutory attorney fees are possible?

_____%

    (b) In cases where statutory attorney fees are possible, please indicate whether your rates are based on market value or reduced market value.

        Market Value   _____
        Reduced Market Value   _____
        Other (specify _____)   _____

19. What potential new sources of funding are you familiar with?

20. Describe efforts your groups has pursued to pool or share resources with others.

21. Has its current level of funding limited your organization's law program in any way? (e.g., kinds of cases it can or cannot undertake, quality of personnel, administrative efficiency, ability to make long range plans, access to technical assistance and data, etc.)

A SPECIAL REQUEST

To enhance our public education program, we would like detailed information about the activities and accomplishments of public interest law programs. Please enclose copies of dockets, brochures, annual reports, or any additional information which will tell us about what you are doing. If you know of other public interest law programs or private firms that have gotten underway recently, please list their names, locations, and a contact name on the back of this questionnaire.

We will also publish a directory of the organizations identified in this survey for public use, which will include the name, address, and phone number of each organization, and an indication of its major program concern(s). Please check below if you do not want this information included in the directory.

_____ Do not include our organization in your directory.

Name of person completing this questionnaire _____
                           Signature _____
                           Title _____

Appendix C

RESPONDENTS TO THE ALLIANCE'S QUESTIONNAIRE SURVEY OF PUBLIC INTEREST LAW CENTERS ORGANIZED BY PRIMARY AREA OF PROGRAMMATIC FOCUS

CLIENT

Children

Advocates for Children of New York
Children's Defense Fund
Children's Rights Project—American Civil Liberties Union
Education Law Center
Institute for Child Advocacy
Juvenile Justice Clinic (Georgetown University Law Center)
Juvenile Law Center of Philadelphia
Legal Services for Children
National Center for Youth Law
National Juvenile Justice Law Center
Public Education Association
Youth Policy and Law Center

Disabled

Advocacy Center for the Elderly and Disabled
Advocacy, Inc.
American Council of the Blind
Bay Area Center for Law and the Deaf
Carolina Legal Assistance—Mental Disability Law Project
Center for Law and Health Sciences (Boston University School of Law)
Community Health Law Project
Disability Rights Center
Disability Rights Education and Defense Fund, Inc.
Mental Health Law Project
National Association of the Deaf Legal Defense Fund
National Center for Law and the Deaf
Santa Clara County Bar Association Mental Health Advocacy Project

153

Untapped Resources, Inc.
Western Law Center for the Handicapped (Loyola Law School)

Employment/Workers

Employment Law Center
Industrial Cooperative Association

Elderly

Legal Counsel for the Elderly
Legal Services for the Elderly
National Senior Citizens Law Center

Gay/Lesbian

American Association for Personal Privacy
Gay/Lesbian Advocates and Defenders
Lambda Legal Defense and Education Fund
Lesbian Rights Project
National Gay Rights Advocates

Minorities

Asian American Legal Defense and Education Fund
Asian Law Caucus
Chicano Education Project
Immigration Law Clinic (Columbia Law School)
Indian Law Resource Center
Mexican American Legal Defense and Educational Fund
NAACP Legal Defense and Education Fund
National Center for Immigration Rights
Native American Rights Fund
Oficina Legal del Pueblo
Puerto Rican Legal Defense and Education Fund, Inc.
Vietnam Veterans Association Legal Services

Poverty

Advocates for Basic Legal Equality
Antioch Poverty Clinic (Antioch Law School)
Appalachian Research and Defense Fund, Inc.
California Rural Legal Assistance
Center for Rural Affairs
Center for Law and Education
Center on Social Welfare Policy and Law
Colorado Coalition of Legal Services Programs
Colorado Lawyers Committee

Council of New York Law Associates
Food Research Action Center
Massachusetts Law Reform Institute
Migrant Legal Action
National Coalition for the Homeless
National Consumer Law Center
National Economic Development and Law Center
National Health Law Program
National Housing Law Project
Project Justice and Equality
Public Advocates
Public Counsel
Southern Poverty Law Center
Urban Legal Clinic (Rutgers Law School)
Western Center on Law and Poverty

CAUSE

Environmental

Connecticut Fund for the Environment
Conservation Law Foundation of New England
Environmental Defense Fund
Legal Environmental Assistance Foundation
National Wildlife Federation
Natural Resources Defense Council
New Jersey Public Interest Research Group
Northwest Environmental Defense Center (Lewis and Clark Law School)
1000 Friends of Oregon
Pacific Northwest Resources Clinic
Sierra Club Legal Defense Fund
Trustees for Alaska

International

Alien Rights Law Project, Washington Lawyers' Committee for Civil Rights Under Law
International Human Rights Law Group
Lawyers Committee for International Human Rights

Media/Communications

Citizens Communication Center
Communications Law Project (UCLA Law School)
Communications Media Center
Media Access Project
Office of Communication (United Church of Christ)

Reporters Committee for Freedom of the Press
Telecommunications Research and Action Center

Multi-issue

Arizona Center for Law in the Public Interest
Business and Professional People for the Public Interest
Center for Constitutional Rights
Center for Law and Social Policy
Center for Law in the Public Interest
Center for Public Representation
Government Accountability Project
Harrison Institute for Public Law
Institute for Public Representation
Massachusetts Public Interest Research Group
Michigan Public Interest Research Group
Minnesota Public Interest Research Group
New Jersey Department of Public Advocates
New York Lawyers in the Public Interest
New York Public Interest Research Group
Public Citizen Litigation Group
Public Interest Law Center of Philadelphia
San Francisco Lawyers Committee for Urban Affairs
Southern Legal Counsel
Trial Lawyers for Public Justice
United States Public Interest Research Group

Appendix D

INDIVIDUALS INTERVIEWED
FOR THIS REPORT

In addition to the Alliance board members, the following individuals were interviewed:

John Adams
Nancy Amidei
Alvin Bronstein
Norman Chachkin
Nancy Drabble
Pablo Eisenberg
Jean Fairfax
Peter Forsythe
Burton Fretz
Lisa Goldberg
Barry Goldstein
Jack Greenberg
Marsha Greenberger
Susan Gross
Morton Halperin
Mary Hanewall
Patricia Hewitt
Leonard Lesser
Elizabeth McCormack

Judge Abner Mikva
Patrick Parenteau
Robert Percival
Carol Pitchersky
Ronald Pollack
Harriet Rabb
Robert Roggeveen
Anthony Roisman
Donald Ross
Roberta Ross
Herman Schwartz
Renee Schwartz
Robert J. Stein
William L. Taylor
Michael Trister
Mary Lynn Walker
Bruce Williams
Roger Willson

Index